Mastering
Expert Systems
with Turbo Prolog

Mastering Expert Systems with Turbo Prolog

Carl Townsend

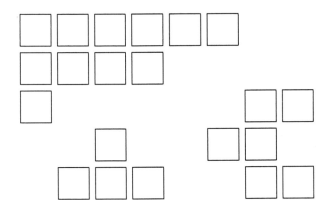

HOWARD W. SAMS & COMPANY

A Division of Macmillan, Inc.
4300 West 62nd Street
Indianapolis, Indiana 46268 USA

FIRST EDITION
SECOND PRINTING—1988

International Standard Book Number: 0-672-22568-9
Library of Congress Catalog Card Number: 86-63288

Acquisitions Editor: *Greg Michael*
Editor: *Susan Pink Bussiere*
Designer: *T. R. Emrick*
Illustrator: *Ralph E. Lund*
Cover Designer: *Keith J. Hampton, Visual Graphic Services*
Cover Illustrator: *Debi Stewart, Visual Graphic Services*
Compositor: *Shepard Poorman Communications,
Indianapolis*

Printed in the United States of America

Trademark Acknowledgments

All terms mentioned in this book that are known to be
trademarks or service marks are listed below. In addition,
terms suspected of being trademarks or service marks have
been appropriately capitalized. Howard W. Sams & Co.
cannot attest to the accuracy of this information. Use of a
term in this book should not be regarded as affecting the
validity of any trademark or service mark.

Arity and Arity Prolog are trademarks of Arity
Corporation.
AT, PC-DOS, and XT are trademarks and IBM is a
registered trademark of International Business Machines,
Inc.
dBASE III is a trademark of Ashton-Tate.
Digital Equipment Corporation (DEC) and VAX are
trademarks of Digital Equipment Corp.
Expert-Ease is a trademark of Expert Software
International.
KEE is a trademark of Intellicorp.
Lotus and 1-2-3 are trademarks of Lotus Development
Corp.
M.1 is a trademark of Teknowledge, Inc.
Personal Consultant is a trademark of Texas Instruments.
Turbo Prolog is a registered trademark of Borland
International.
Whodunit is a registered trademark of Selchow & Righter.
WORD is a trademark and Microsoft and MS-DOS are
registered trademarks of Microsoft Corp.
WordStar is a registered trademark of MicroPro
International Corp.

Contents

Contents

Introduction

Mastering Expert Systems with Turbo Prolog is an introductory tutorial for those interested in designing expert systems, particularly with Turbo Prolog. The major objectives include the following:

- explore the current status of expert system design on personal computers
- introduce you to Prolog, particularly Turbo Prolog, as an expert system design tool
- describe the basics of logic programming using examples and easy-to-understand concepts
- explain in detail the design concepts of a Turbo Prolog expert system
- provide a sample of a complete diagnostic expert system written in Turbo Prolog
- provide information on resources for those wanting to pursue expert systems in more depth

The reader is assumed to have experience with DOS and access to Turbo Prolog, but only a minimum of programming expertise is required.

Until 1985, the Prolog language was almost exclusively used by the academic community and the research departments of major corporations. With a few exceptions, it was not considered a productive language tool for the personal computer. Versions for personal computers, where they did exist, were too expensive, slow, and poorly designed to be very practical. The few resources available were written primarily for experienced programmers and the academic community.

Today, this is rapidly changing. Within the space of a few months, several excellent versions of Prolog for the personal computer emerged on the market. Turbo Prolog was one of these products, and gained a rapid following because of its low cost and excellent design. But with these new tools, unfortunately, there were few resources available on how to use any type of Prolog for productive expert system design.

Mastering Expert Systems with Turbo Prolog is a response to that need. The basic concepts of Prolog are developed and the design of a complete Turbo Prolog expert system for diagnosing problems in personal computers is explained.

The text is designed to be as nontechnical as possible. Academic concepts and terms are omitted to keep the text clear and readable, and the language is as close as possible to that in the Turbo Prolog manual. A glossary of terms is included for those new to Prolog and expert systems. For readers interested in pursuing more technical aspects of Prolog, an annotated Bibliography gives information on resources.

The book is divided into two parts. Part 1 is a basic tutorial for the Turbo Prolog language as applied to expert system design. This section was not intended as a complete tutorial for Turbo Prolog; it is primarily directed to Prolog concepts necessary in the design of expert systems. If you haven't used Turbo Prolog, this section should help demystify basic concepts such as backtracking, the cut, and recursion. If you already have a familiarity with Prolog, you may be tempted to skip this section. If possible, however, at least skim this material and become acquainted with the terminology. In addition to many of the features of the standard C & M Prolog, Turbo Prolog also has C-like features, which have both advantages and disadvantages. (Refer to appendix A.)

Part 2 is an expert system tutorial. You will learn about the types of knowledge representation used in expert system design, how to represent knowledge, and other introductory concepts. Many of the more technical aspects are omitted to keep the text as clear and readable as possible. This section includes the complete design of an expert system to diagnose and repair IBM PC compatible computers. The complete program listing for this expert system is in appendix B.

Acknowledgments

I would like to express my appreciation to Albert Holt and others at Borland International, Susan Pink Bussiere of Techright, and the staff at Howard W. Sams who helped in various ways during the writing of this book.

part 1

Turbo Prolog and Expert System Fundamentals

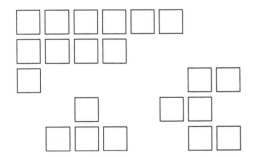

Part 1

Turbo Prolog and Expert
System Fundamentals

chapter $\boxed{1}$

Fundamentals of Expert Systems

☐ At a medical convention before hundreds of physicians, a young doctor took the podium and listed a series of symptoms for a patient he was treating. After he had finished reading the list, he asked the physicians in the audience for diseases that might be related to these symptoms. First one hand was raised, then a second. After fifteen minutes, the prestigious group had suggested five diseases that might be symptomatic to the given indications. The young man smiled, then listed over forty diseases selected as symptomatic by an expert system he had queried. The expert system had outperformed the collected knowledge of over 900 physicians.

This young man was not implying that an expert system has more wisdom than a human doctor or that an expert system can replace a human doctor in the diagnosis of diseases. The young man was implying, however, that it is very difficult for the mind of a medical doctor to store and manage the knowledge required to make intelligent medical decisions in today's world. An expert system is a tool that can help a doctor manage knowledge and make decisions. It does not replace the doctor.

The same problem exists in almost any type of professional discipline today—law, engineering, operations management, oil exploration, career counseling, and psychology. We have accumulated a large amount of knowledge in each of these fields, but it is beyond the ability of professionals to use all of this knowledge effectively in making decisions.

Expert systems are tools that can help a human expert make better decisions and, in some cases, help a nonprofessional make limited decisions without the help of an expert.

What Is an Expert System?

Expert systems are a class of computer hardware and software that can help advise, diagnose, analyze, consult, and categorize. They are tools for problems that normally require the use of a human expert, professional, or specialist. Unlike traditional computer hardware and software that attempts to solve problems using defined procedures, expert systems attempt to solve problems in specific disciplines using deductive reasoning. As a result, expert systems are capable of solving problems that are unstructured and poorly defined.

The study of expert systems is one branch of artificial intelligence, which is a branch of computer science. Artificial intelligence is primarily concerned with knowledge representation, problem solving, learning, robotics, and the development of computers that can speak and understand more natural (humanlike) languages. Refer to figure 1.1. Edward Feigenbaum, a leading researcher in expert systems, defines an expert system as "a computer program that uses knowledge and inference procedures to solve problems that are difficult enough to require significant human expertise for their solution."

Expert systems simulate the problem-solving process of human experts. In building an expert system, the knowledge of one or more experts must be captured and stored in such a way that it can be used to make decisions. The expert system actually contains the knowledge of one or more human experts, and draws on this knowledge to solve problems. As we shall see later in this chapter and the next, this concept is a dramatically different problem-solving approach than that used by traditional computer programs. Unlike traditional systems, expert systems can solve problems even when input information is missing or uncertain.

Expert systems are almost always designed to solve problems in a single discipline, topical area, or region of knowledge. This is referred to as the *domain* of the expert system. All of the expert systems that provide useful expertise today function in a very narrow domain. The limits of this domain must be carefully defined when the expert system is designed and used.

The Importance of Expert Systems

The importance of expert systems as tools for human experts is increasing. They will eventually emerge as consumer products for nonexperts in many domains as the price of access to human experts continues to increase. In 1985, informal surveys indicated that approximately fifty percent of Fortune 500 companies were investing in production-type

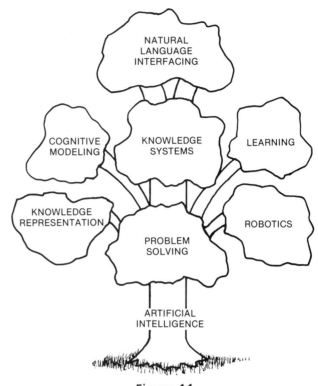

Figure 1.1
The field of artificial intelligence

expert systems (explained in chapter 14), and about ten percent had products under development. The actual figures, however, are probably much higher. Most companies pursuing research in this area consider it highly proprietary. You may find a statistic that indicates a company purchased an expert system tool or language, but finding out how the language or tool is being used by the company is quite another task.

Types of Expert Systems

Expert systems can be used in applications involving diagnosis, prediction, consultation, control, planning, instruction, and interpretation. Let us look briefly at each of these.

Diagnosis

Diagnosis still remains the primary application of expert systems, particularly for personal computers. Diagnostic systems can be used to repair computers, diagnose medical illnesses, repair diesel locomotives, and determine food allergies. Primary requirements are a consistent relationship between symptoms and causes, and the ability to identify these relationships. The primary difficulties are the masking of symptoms by other symptoms, intermittent symptoms, unaccessible data, and lack of knowledge about relationships of symptoms (faults) and causes.

Interpretation

Interpretive systems analyze data to determine its meaning. An example might be a system that analyzes mass spectrometer data to determine one or more chemical structures. The requirements are a known and consistent interpretation from a given set of data. In most cases, the system must be rigorously complete in that a solution is only provided if the system is absolutely sure of the interpretation. Primary difficulties are incomplete input data, long reasoning chains, unreliable data, and reasoning with contradictory data.

Prediction

Expert systems can be used to predict the weather from data about the temperature, barometric pressure, wind direction, wind velocity, and current cloud formations. Surprisingly, small weather prediction systems on personal computers can be quite accurate.

Monitoring and Control

Complex systems such as nuclear power plants, medical monitoring systems, and aircraft traffic control need to make quick decisions from complex data. Often a human cannot analyze the data fast enough to make adequate decisions. In other cases, twenty-four-hour monitoring is necessary, and it is not always possible to consult an expert when decisions must be made. Expert systems can be used to monitor complex variables, summarize the results, and suggest a decision for a human expert.

A medical expert system that monitors a patient during an operation could automatically control the injection of an intravenous drug, without human intervention, based on predefined symptoms and rules. This would leave the doctors and nurses free for the more critical aspects of the operation.

Another type of control involves financial decisions within a company. For example, a corporation could define a series of rules that determine the eligibility of travel expenses for reimbursement. These rules, in turn, could be used in the creation of an expert system. When a salesperson returns from a trip, expense categories and values are entered for each day, and the expert system could determine the amount of corporate reimbursement using predetermined company rules.

The primary difficulty in the design of monitoring and control systems is that the system must function in real time. Input data arrives at the system from sensors and decisions must be made quickly. Expert systems today are rarely known for their speed, and the meaning of a signal from a sensor could be time dependent. Sensor data that is within limits at one time in a cycle may be dangerously out of limits at another point in the cycle.

Planning

A plan is a procedure or program of actions that can be carried out to achieve a specified goal. Planning means to create a plan. Planning systems can be used to configure (plan) computer systems and networks. In preparing proposals, computer salespeople for minicomputers and mainframe systems must consider each installation as unique. There are hundreds or thousands of variables to consider, all of which affect the final price and delivery schedule. Expert systems can be used to ensure that all variables are considered and no detail is omitted from the final proposal. Even small expert systems on a personal computer can be valuable in ensuring that the proper hardware and software is selected to meet the specific demands of the customer.

A planning system reasons about time-dependent variables. The system must be able to deal with chronological events and their relationships. In almost all cases, you are dealing with incomplete information. You are hypothesizing futures, then studying what goal state will result from these hypotheses.

Planning expert systems can support career counseling, nutritional analysis, investment counseling, operations management, and psychiatric counseling. A corporate executive trying to make a decision on a merger or acquisition could store a battery of knowledge on the problem, then use the expert system to sort through hundreds of facts and make the most intelligent decision.

Instruction

In general, when you want to learn something about a subject, you go to an expert. In the same way, an expert system can be used to teach you something about the subject in which it is an expert. By changing the input conditions, you can affect the output. For example, if you are studying management, you might want to simulate the operation of a dummy corporation. Using spreadsheets and data, you try to make decisions on your own. After each decision, you could use an expert system to make the decisions from the same data as well as explore how the expert system makes each decision. You could then compare the decisions of the expert system with the decisions you made on your own. As you explore your own successes and failures with the dummy corporation, you will gain better insights into what makes a corporation successful.

Applications for Expert Systems

Most expert systems can actually be classified as more than one type. A diagnostic medical system for diseases, for example, might monitor certain patient variables, diagnose what is wrong, and help the doctor plan a strategy.

Although the use of expert systems with personal computers is still very limited, this is certain to change soon. Hardware capabilities are rapidly increasing while hardware costs are decreasing. Better development tools are emerging. Scientists are gaining more insights into the theories and concepts necessary to build effective systems. The basic principles used in developing these larger systems are already being applied to the development of personal expert systems.

Let's look at a few examples of successful expert systems. All of these are quite large, running on minicomputers or mainframes. They represent only a sample of how expert systems are being used productively today. Many of the better applications remain highly proprietary. In part 2, we will look closer at what you can do with a personal computer and Turbo Prolog.

MYCIN

The most famous expert system is probably MYCIN. MYCIN was developed at Stanford University during the seventies for the diagnosis and treatment of meningitis and bacteremia infections. The system currently performs at the level of a human expert, and is a well accepted diagnostic expert system in the medical community. Modified versions of MYCIN are being developed for other medical domains: PUFF diagnoses pulmonary diseases and ONCOCIN has been developed for cancer diagnosis.

XCON

Digital Equipment Corporation (DEC) uses its XCON (for eXpert CONfigurator) expert system to configure VAX minicomputers for customers. XCON was originally called R1 and was developed at Carnegie-Mellon University in Pittsburgh in 1979. (There is a legend that the original name came from the engineers. One complained that he never could spell engineering and now he "are one.")

In 1979, over 400 components were required to configure a typical VAX-11/780 computer system. DEC tried to develop a computer program that would configure systems, but the complex parts list and the interrelationship of parts were constantly changing, making program development impossible. John McDermott at Carnegie-Mellon thought the project would be ideal for an expert system.

XCON eventually moved to commercial use at DEC. The abilities of XCON today far exceed the skill of any human expert, and it would be virtually impossible for DEC to return XCON's task to any human experts. XCON has saved DEC millions of dollars.

A highly trained technical salesperson is required to use XCON effectively. This person collects data from the customer on the computer equipment, printers, and other peripherals desired. Other relevant data is also collected (for example, air conditioning data and the size of the doors to the computer room). XCON then goes to work to define all the necessary components and the best layout for the room, and eventually prints a component list and the physical layout. Any design problems are identified for correction.

PROSPECTOR

PROSPECTOR was developed in the late seventies by a team at Stanford Research International (SRI) that included Peter Hart, Richard Duda, R. Reboh, K. Konolige, M. Einandi, and P. Barrett. It was designed to assist geologists in the early stages of investigation for ore-grade deposits. The development was funded by the U.S. Geological Survey and the National Science Foundation. PROSPECTOR was eventually quite successful, finding a $100 million molybdenum ore deposit that had eluded nine experts.

PROSPECTOR can accept raw data from magnometers carried by airplanes, from Landstat photos, and from the analysis of core samples obtained by geologists. It can also accept graphic input.

How an Expert System Works

Expert systems can be applied to problems that are primarily solved using formal reasoning and have no defined procedure. You solve the problem through a dialog, or "consultation," with the expert system. In a simple expert system, you answer each question with "yes," "no," or "why?" The "why" answer is used if you do not understand the reasoning of the system and want to know how the expert system "thinks."

For example, a simple expert system that diagnoses problems in an IBM PC compatible computer system is shown in figure 1.2. The Turbo Prolog listing for this program will be developed later in this book, but for now let's look at how you would use the system.

When the program is started, you are asked a series of questions. You answer based on your observation of the computer's operation. The program may suggest further tests, and then ask for the results of these tests. Eventually, the expert system is able to make a diagnosis of what is wrong with the computer.

Notice several things about this dialog:

1. The answers are primarily yes or no, but in some cases the user is asked to make a selection from a list, or menu, of possibilities.

2. The questions always relate to symptoms, or observable behavior.

3. The user interface is a dialog, similar to a consulting session.

In more complex systems, the user might enter a number to indi-

```
What basic type of problem do you have?
    1) Startup problem
    2) Run problem
    3) Display problem
    4) Keyboard problem
    5) Printer problem
SELECT: 2
Is the ambient temperature near the computer <= 90 degrees
        Fahrenheit and >= 60 degrees Fahrenheit, are all fans
        operational, and are all ventilation openings unblocked
        (y/n) ? y
What type of run problem are you experiencing?
    1) Computer locks up but power stays up; keyboard is dead.
    2) Computer drops power, turning itself off.
    3) Parity error messages.
    4) Computer crashes when turning on peripheral.
    5) Erratic operation or intermittent failures.
    6) Problems in operating one specific program.
    7) Hard disk problems.
    8) Floppy disk problems.
    9) Overheating.
SELECT: 8
What are the disk symptoms?
    1) The floppy disk is dead--no load light when accessed.
    2) The following message is displayed: "Not ready reading drive
        X. Abort, Retry, Ignore?"
    3) Does not read or write properly.
    4) Reads correctly, but does not write.
    5) The disk drive makes an unusual sound.
    6) Difficult to load or unload disks.
SELECT: 4
Check the disk visually for physical damage.
Does the disk appear okay (y/n) ? y
Is the write-protect hole on the disk uncovered (y/n) ? y
Try removing all resident programs by starting without the
        AUTOEXEC.BAT file (RENAME it and reboot).
Does the problem persist (y/n)? y
Do you have a second disk drive or access to another compatible
        computer (y/n) ? y
Does the disk work the same way on the other drive (y/n) ? y
Recover the data you can from the disk, then reformat and test
        the disk. If it fails again, destroy or replace the disk.
        You should probably change disk brands if the problem
        happens with several disks of the same brand.
Would you like another consultation (y/n) ? n
```

Figure 1.2
Dialog with a Turbo Prolog expert system

cate a confidence in the statement being true. (0 is false or no; 1 is an extremely high confidence in the statement being true or yes. This is discussed in chapter 19.) There may also be a way to skip questions if the answer is not known. With some systems, the answers may be quite "free form." For example, the system may begin by asking *What is wrong with the computer?* The user describes the symptoms (such as *The computer does not boot*) and the dialog continues.

Problem Solving with Expert Systems

Traditional computer programs are developed by programmers who are skilled at adapting the procedures used to solve a specific problem into a language that a computer can understand. The procedure is often called an algorithm, and (if correct) always produces a correct answer from a defined input.

For example, if you want a loan to purchase a car, you can calculate the monthly payment from the amount you need to borrow and the interest rate. There is a definite procedure, or algorithm, to make this calculation. If the input data is correct, the output answer will always be correct if the correct algorithm is used. With the same input data, the output answer is always the same. A programmer could write a computer program to implement the procedure and make the calculation. Then, using different input data, the same program (and procedure) could be used to solve many problems.

Expert systems, in contrast, have no defined procedure that is stored as part of the program. Instead of calculating an answer using a predefined procedure, the expert system tries to use what it knows about the subject to define a procedure to achieve the specified goal—a process the human expert calls formal reasoning.

Another way we could look at how an expert system solves a problem is to view it as charting a course though a problem space to a specific goal, as shown in figure 1.3. A *node* is any defined point in the problem space and the final goal is the final node. There are also many subgoals within the problem space, and each is represented by a node. In a traditional computer system, there is a single path through the problem space to the goal and the path is specifically defined before the problem can be solved.

In an expert system, there is no predefined path through the problem space. In fact, part of the problem is to define this path. There is no guarantee that a path exists through the problem space to the final goal. A *heuristic* is a rule of thumb that can be used to find one of many paths, the most efficient path, or the only path to the final goal.

Knowledge engineers (not programmers) are used to develop expert systems. They are skilled at observing and analyzing the methods used by human experts to solve problems in a particular discipline. These methods, or heuristics, are stored as part of the data. The knowledge engineer is more concerned with developing heuristics than algorithms.

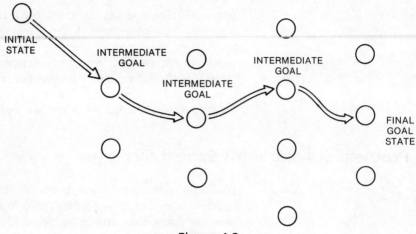

Figure 1.3
Charting through a problem space

For example, imagine Sherlock Holmes trying to solve a case. He collects hundreds of clues (for example, the suspect has a black hat and the suspect's fingers have calluses). The police may also have hundreds of facts, but what distinguishes the expertise of Holmes and the police in solving the crime? Holmes is able to use other rules, or heuristics, to determine what is important and what is not important, working through the mass of information to the eventual solution.

Problem-Solving Strategies

Expert systems have another distinction from traditional computer programs. Whereas traditional programs process variables and values, expert systems process symbols. In this sense, the expert system is much like the human mind.

Humans use analogy, formal reasoning, numerical analysis, intuition, and common sense to solve problems. When a problem must be solved using numerical analysis alone, the traditional computer program is faster, more reliable, and more efficient than the human mind.

In contrast, the human mind is most efficient when using symbolic processing. Even before we are born, our eyes begin to interpret visual images, storing these as patterns in the brain. We eventually learn to identify object symbols that are stored (for example, mother, father, tree, and dog) and their relationships. An *object* is a real-world entity. A *symbol* is an arbitrary sign that represents an object.

The following, for example, is an expression of a symbolic relationship:

```
John likes Sue.
```

This could be stored as a meaningful fact in the human mind or in an expert system. It could not be stored as a fact in a traditional computer program.

We can process information about new data by comparing it with other objects that share the same relationship. For example, suppose we know that John likes Sue and we know the meaning of "likes." If someone tells us that Jack likes Mary, we know what it means even though the objects are different. In this way we can learn new facts.

The human mind develops heuristics (or rules for solving problems) by grouping knowledge that is related. When faced with a new problem, we use a pattern-matching process to find out if there are other objects that share the same relationship. For example, if a car does not start, an expert first tries to find the defective subsystem. The expert knows it is probably the electrical or fuel system. After the subsystem is identified, the next task is to identify the component within the subsystem. The expert is trying to use a heuristic to reduce the size of the problem space. If the car does not start, there is no sense checking the water because the cooling system is not used to start the car. Solving the problem is essentially a pattern-matching process. If the headlights are dim, the expert is aware that most likely the battery connections are bad or the battery is dead. The expert matches the condition to previously stored patterns, working through the solution process until the cause is discovered.

To build an expert system to diagnose automotive problems, the knowledge engineer must first identify the heuristics used by the expert. The expert system must duplicate the same pattern-matching process when it solves a problem. The knowledge engineer also recognizes that this can only be accomplished to a limited degree. The human expert uses formal reasoning, analogy, intuition, common sense, and procedural methods. Expert systems today can use only formal reasoning and limited procedural analysis.

Exercises

Note: Answers to all exercise questions are in appendix C.

1. Identify a person you consider an expert in a specific field. Why do you consider that person an expert?

2. In what way are the skills of the knowledge engineer different from that of a programmer? How are they similar?

3. In each of the following applications, tell whether a traditional computer system or knowledge system is more applicable and why.

    a. General ledger system.

    b. Traffic control at an intersection. (A real-time system that uses sensors to measure traffic flow, then adjusts the sequencing for different traffic conditions during the day and week.)

c. Washing machine repair. (A central system for repairmen on routes to use for repairing several dozen washing machine models.)

d. Sales order system.

e. Toxic waste analysis and control. (A nuclear power plant has several toxic wastes, and must create a system for emergency response when one of the waste disposal systems is out of control.)

f. Poison control center. (People call with questions and the person at the center must provide answers very rapidly.)

chapter $\boxed{2}$

Introduction to Expert System Languages

☐ Expert systems can be developed in almost any computer language, but some languages are far better for expert system applications than others. This chapter explains why some languages are better than others for designing expert systems and introduces one of these languages, Prolog.

Procedural and Data-Driven Control Flow

Almost all of the languages used with computers during the last few decades were primarily designed for procedural processing. In procedural processing, you must first define an algorithm that can solve the problem. The program is then written to implement the algorithm. After the program is written, it can execute the same procedure many times to solve problems with different input data. The problem solution is a linear process, executed one step at a time.

Procedural languages distinguish between the program and data. The programmer defines the procedure and the control structure for the solution of the problem. The program uses the data for the solution of the problem. By changing the data, you can solve new problems with the same procedure.

FORTRAN, BASIC, C, COBOL, Pascal, and even assembly-level languages are all examples of procedural languages. These languages are excellent tools for numerical processing, but they are dramatically inefficient when used in the development of expert systems.

Most of the current hardware architecture used by mainframes, minicomputers, and personal computers is designed to support the use of procedural languages. In this architecture (*von Neumann architecture,* named after the inventor), a single block of memory is used for both the program and the data. The computer cannot distinguish between memory used for either.

Any program may be data to another program. When writing a program, a programmer uses an editor or word processor. At this time, the "program" is data to the editor program. After it is edited, the data becomes a program. The computer executes a program in a linear fashion. It starts reading the first instruction at a specific point in memory, interprets it, and executes it. The computer then reads the next instruction.

Procedural languages and von Neumann architectures are inefficient for expert systems. In solving a problem with an expert system, there is no defined or fixed procedure. In fact, the problem may be unstructured and the procedure to solve it may be unknown. What is known about the domain is stored as data and the program must use this data to develop its own procedure, which can vary each time the program is executed. Formal reasoning is used to obtain the problem solution and there is more emphasis on symbolic, rather than numerical, processing.

To write an expert system, you describe what you know about the domain as facts and the relationship between these facts. The computer has the job of both finding a procedure to solve the problem and solving the problem. The computer primarily uses formal reasoning.

Expert systems, in contrast with traditional systems, are more often developed using *data-driven languages*. These languages make no distinction between program and data, and are capable of symbolic processing. The data about the domain determines how the problem will be solved. LISP and Prolog are examples of data-driven languages.

Instead of a programmer, a knowledge engineer develops and maintains the system. The knowledge engineer has the job of converting the expert's knowledge into a systematic structure that can be interpreted by Prolog.

The most efficient hardware for expert systems utilizes parallel processing and is highly interactive. Parallel processing implies that the computer can do several things at the same time. The computer may have many processors, and each works on the same problem at the same time. Computers that use parallel processing, however, are still very expensive. In this book, the primary emphasis is on the Turbo Prolog language, which is a data-driven language for IBM PC compatible computers. IBM PC compatible computers use the more traditional von Neumann architecture, but they are far less expensive than systems designed for parallel processing. In addition, you still have an advantage in that you can use the computer for numerical processing as well. Table 2.1 details the differences between procedural and expert systems.

Table 2.1
Procedural Systems and Expert Systems

Procedural System (Traditional)	Expert System (Declarative)
Uses previously defined procedures to solve problems	Uses heuristics to solve problems
Uses numerical processing	Uses formal reasoning
von Neumann architecture	Not von Neumann architecture
Uses linear processing	Uses parallel and interactive processing
Developed and maintained by programmers	Developed and maintained by knowledge engineers
Structured design	Interactive and cyclic design

Compiler or Interpreter?

A computer processor cannot directly execute a program written in a computer language. The instructions written by the programmer (the source program) must be converted into a form the processor can understand before they are executed. This is accomplished with either a compiler or an interpreter.

Interpreters remain in memory with the user's program, and use the program as input data. Each time the program runs, each statement is interpreted, converted to the machine's language, and then executed. As a result, an interpreter is always slow because it must both interpret and execute the program each time the program runs. Using an interpreter also requires plenty of memory. The interpreter, your program, and your data must all be in the computer's memory at the same time. Also, the user always needs the interpreter to use the program. If the program is sold as a product, the user will need to purchase the interpreter to use the product.

There are some major advantages, however, to using an interpreter. The program can be developed quickly. The developer does not need to wait for the program to compile (as with a compiler) each time the source program is changed. When the program is executing, it can be stopped at any point and variables can be observed and changed. The popular BASICA, which comes with most IBM PC computers, and dBASE III are interpreters.

Compilers read a source program and convert it to the machine's language, storing it on disk in an executable form (EXE or COM is the extension). After the process of compiling is completed, the program can be executed at any time by calling it from the disk directly. The language and compiler are not needed again unless the source program is changed and must be compiled again.

Compiled programs execute much faster than interpreted programs. Less computer memory is needed. The user does not need the language compiler to use the resulting program. Compilers, then, can be used to develop products that are marketed and sold to users. Almost all application programs (for example, Lotus 1-2-3 and Microsoft WORD) are developed with compilers. They are sold as executable programs; you do not get the source code.

Turbo Prolog is a compiler. After an expert system is developed with Turbo Prolog, it is converted to an executable program that can be marketed to an end user. The end user does not need to purchase Turbo Prolog. At the same time, however, you have many of the advantages of an interpreter. You can develop programs quickly, trace programs as they execute, and switch from editing mode to execution mode very quickly.

High-Level Languages Versus Low-Level Languages

Computer languages can be classed as high-level languages or low-level languages. In a high-level language, a single statement translates into many instructions at the machine-language level. dBASE III is a very high-level language. BASIC, COBOL, Pascal, and FORTRAN are all high-level languages. High-level languages are much closer to natural languages in form and structure than low-level languages. Thus, it is easier to read and interpret a high-level language.

Low-level languages are languages in which a single statement in the source program translates into a single machine instruction. For example, assembly-level languages are low-level languages because a single statement or line of code translates into a single machine instruction. The C language is fairly low level. A programmer can do more with a low-level language than with a high-level language. Using a low-level language is somewhat like driving a sports car; the road will seem rougher and it takes more work than using a sedan, but you have more control over the car's performance.

Programs can be developed faster using high-level languages. They are also easier to debug. Using high-level languages, a programmer can develop very complex programs in a relatively short time. For example, I can write a program in dBASE III (a very high-level language) that will do the same thing as a program written in BASIC (a moderately high-level language), yet it takes only one-tenth of the time to write the program in dBASE III in comparison with BASIC. The disadvantage of high-level languages is that the programmer is bound by the constraints of the language.

Prolog is considered a high-level language, even though it is non-procedural in form. The developer works at a level closer to natural languages than with many computer languages, and programs are developed in a relatively short time. In contrast, LISP is considered a low-level expert system language. Refer to figure 2.1. If you need the power and control of a low-level language, you should consider LISP. If you are just starting with expert systems and you consider LISP too complex and time consuming, Prolog can give you a lot of power for a little work. You can also write Prolog interpreters in LISP.

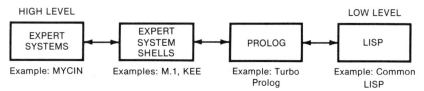

Figure 2.1
Expert system languages and tools

Requirements of an Expert System Language

To build an expert system, certain language requirements are necessary:

1. The language should support data-driven structures.

2. The language must support symbolic processing. In other words, you should be able to use symbols, and not just numeric values, to represent objects. You must be able to do formal reasoning with the symbolic variables.

3. The language must support list processing. You should be able to build linked-list symbolic structures with hierarchical relationships, as shown in figure 2.2.

4. The language must support recursion (described in chapter 10).

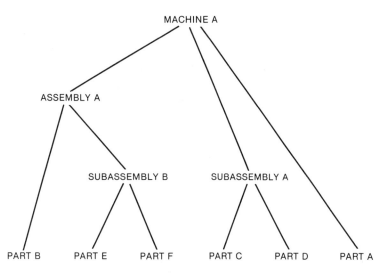

Figure 2.2
A hierarchical relationship

Expert System Languages

Prolog, LISP, and FORTH are all data-driven languages capable of symbolic processing. Most artificial intelligence development is accomplished in the LISP language, which could be considered a low-level interpreter. Various versions of LISP are available. Because LISP is an interpreter, the user will need a copy of LISP to run any expert system developed with the language.

FORTH is an interesting language for artificial intelligence work from several aspects. It is both a high-level and low-level language, and is more technically called a threaded interpretive language. High-level routines are written using low-level routines, enabling you to create a high-level language based on your specific needs. FORTH is faster than an interpreter, but lacks the speed of a true compiler. The user will need a copy of FORTH to execute an application program.

One of the most popular FORTH expert systems for personal computers is Jack Park's Expert System Toolkit, available from Mountain View Press (MVP). Although MVP's version of FORTH uses a special disk format, a version of the same system is available that runs under F83, a FORTH version that is in the public domain and uses the MS-DOS file format. FORTH expert systems do have disadvantages: they still lack a good editor, programs cannot be compiled for a user who does not have FORTH, their speed is slow, memory requirements are extensive, and the user needs quite a bit of programming expertise to use the expert system.

Prolog is a high-level language that is specifically designed for expert system development. Prolog is the language chosen by Japanese developers for their fifth-generation computers. Prolog can be written in LISP or FORTH, but in either case it would share the interpretive nature of these languages. In short, you needed plenty of memory and a lot of processing power to do anything useful. Turbo Prolog is written in C and assembly language, and is a true compiler.

Perhaps more than anything else, the lack of an adequate language hindered the development of expert systems for productive applications on the personal computer. Today, several powerful Prolog compilers are available. In 1985, the Arity Prolog compiler was marketed. Borland's Turbo Prolog compiler emerged a few months later, in May of 1986. Today, many Prolog compilers are available. For the first time, a user can compile a true expert system—with hundreds of rules—that will function on a personal computer.

Expert System Shells

At a still higher level are expert system *shells,* many of which are available for the personal computer. Expert system shells (or *tools,* as they are often called), contain specific strategies for knowledge representation (described in part 2), inference, and control. Elementary structures for modeling specific types of domains are often included, as well as user interface constructs and editors. The user only needs to add the knowledge for the domain and the system is ready to use.

In the first chapter, for example, the MYCIN expert system was described. The nucleus of this system eventually became EMYCIN, an expert system shell. This was used to create new expert systems such as PUFF and SACON and eventually evolved to M.l, Tecknowledge's expert system shell that is now available for the personal computer. Today, many expert system shells for the personal computer are available: KEE, M.1., Texas Instrument's Personal Consultant, Expert-Ease, and others.

Shells can be written in almost any lower-level language, such as C or LISP. They are more expensive than a language, but they often save the user in development time. As we shall see in part 2, a good expert system shell should offer many features—such as multiple search strategies, multiple knowledge representation methods, support of certainty factors, tracing, and acceptance of real-time input data. It is unreasonable to expect a personal computer expert system to support too many features. As a result, a developer chooses the proper shell for a specific expert system by starting with the problem and working backward, defining the specific features needed. After these are defined, the developer then tries to find an appropriate shell.

Languages, in contrast, support many features. It is up to the developer, however, to write the code for the specific features desired. Prolog, as one of the highest-level expert system languages, offers many advantages from this perspective.

Prolog

Prolog's power is in its ability to infer (derive by reasoning) facts from other facts. This is a distinctly different process than numerical calculations. A numerical processor can calculate the average of a set of input numbers. The average is something new, something not entered into the computer by the user. If this same user enters a hundred addresses, the computer is unable to do anything more with the addresses. They can be sorted or retrieved in any order, but the addresses still remain just that. The computer can tell you nothing about the relationship of the addresses; the computer can only see the addresses as numeric or string variables, not as symbolic objects that have relationships.

In contrast, with Prolog the user can enter non-numeric data to a computer and the computer can deduce new facts (symbolic relationships) from the input data. The process, as we will see, is essentially a pattern-matching process using formal rules.

The name *Prolog* is taken from the phrase *programming in logic*. The language was originally developed in early 1972 by Alain Colmerauer and P. Roussel at the University of Marseilles. The first Prolog compiler was developed at the University of Edinburgh. Prolog is now an international computer language used by expert system developers around the world. Japan's fifth-generation project has adopted Prolog as the basic language for the hardware they are developing.

Programming in Prolog is a completely different experience from using a procedural language. If you have spent decades learning procedural languages, you will have to go through an "unlearning" experience before you can begin to get proficient in Prolog. You will keep trying to apply procedural concepts to your programs and you will have difficulty converting data into a form that adequately supports the problem-solving process. There is an advantage, however, in learning this new language: you will be able to apply the computer to the solution of new problems that are not adaptable to solution using traditional languages.

To write a Prolog expert system program there are essentially four steps:

1. Define the goal.
2. Define the domain.
3. Define the objects in the domain and the facts about these objects.
4. Specify the rules about the facts and their relationships.

Prolog has a few disadvantages and it would not be fair to continue without mentioning these. First, the order of the rules and facts is important to the meaning. Prolog is not truly nonprocedural. Second, all rules must reside in the computer's memory. The number of rules the expert system can use is limited by the memory size of the computer. With most versions of Prolog (including Turbo Prolog), there are methods by which you can use the disk as an extension of memory, but this alternative virtually ensures a very slow program. Later, as you learn more of the language, you will understand other disadvantages.

Remember also that the computer is no more intelligent than the programmer. If the system seems to simulate an expert, it is because an expert existed first and a knowledge engineer knew how to code into a formal system the way the expert solves problems. This process is not always easy.

Exercises

1. In each of the following cases, is the language declarative or procedural?

    a. COBOL

    b. Pascal

    c. LISP

    d. Smalltalk

    e. FORTH

    f. BASIC

    g. dBASE III

    h. Prolog

    i. C

2. Why has Prolog been so slow to emerge as a strong application language on personal computers? Will this change now? (Why or why not?)

3. Is it more difficult for a competent programmer to learn Prolog than to learn another procedural language? (Why or why not?)

chapter $\boxed{3}$

Using Turbo Prolog

☐ Turbo Prolog contains most of the features of the Prolog described in "Programming in Prolog" by Clocksin and Mellish. It is a compiler, and for this reason functions much faster than a Prolog interpreter. Turbo Prolog is a practical tool for developing expert systems on IBM PC compatible computers, and contains the following features:

- You can compile standalone programs that will execute without any Turbo Prolog run-time support. These can be sold or distributed to users, without royalty support to a third party.

- Turbo Prolog supports a full complement of standard predicates for many functions, such as cursor control (graphics), sound, and windows.

- Turbo Prolog can be interfaced to other languages (for example, C and assembly) to provide additional procedural support.

- Unlike most Prologs (including the Clocksin and Mellish version), variables are typed or "declared" (explained in chapter 4). This provides more secure development control and better debugging, and minimizes memory requirements.

- Predicates for random file access are provided.

- Both integer and real arithmetic are supported.

Requirements

Turbo Prolog requires an IBM compatible computer with a minimum of 384K of memory space. In normal operation, five files are used:

PROLOG.EXE   Main program file

PROLOG.OVL   Extension of the program file

PROLOG.SYS   Defines the configuration for the system

PROLOG.ERR   Error message file

PROLOG.HLP   Help message file

The program will execute using only the PROLOG.EXE and PRO-LOG.OVL files. In this case, a default configuration is used, error messages are numeric codes only, and help messages are not available. If you plan to run external programs within Turbo Prolog, you will also need the DOS COMMAND.COM program on the directory specified by the Setup menu.

If you plan to compile Turbo Prolog programs to run external to Turbo Prolog (without the use of the PROLOG.EXE file), you will also need the INIT.OBJ file and PROLOG.LIB, the library file used during the link process.

Loading Turbo Prolog

To use Turbo Prolog, you first load the program:

```
C>Prolog
```

Press the Enter key. Turbo Prolog loads and displays the copyright screen with a request to press the space bar key. Pressing this key completes the startup procedure, displaying a menu bar and four windows: editor, dialog, message, and trace. Refer to figure 3.1. The editor window is used to enter or change programs. During program execution, consultation (input and output) is through the dialog window. The message window keeps you aware of processing activity and the trace window is useful for debugging.

The menu bar at the top displays seven options:

Run   Run a compiled program

Compile   Compile a program in memory for execution

Edit   Enter or change a program in memory

Options   Select the type of compile

Files   Load a program from disk to memory or save a program in memory to the disk

Setup   Change the setup parameters and save the new
           parameters

Quit   Exit Turbo Prolog

To select a menu option, enter the first letter of the desired option or move the cursor to the desired option and press Enter. The default selection on startup is Run, which is of little use because there is no program compiled at starting time. In general, the first option you will use is Edit or Files.

To enter a new program, select the Edit option. The cursor will move to the editor work area and you can begin to enter the program. If you want to load a program that is already stored on disk, select the Files option and then the Load option. Enter the name of the file with the desired directory path (omit the PRO file extension). The program will load to the editor work area.

When the program is ready to run, you can exit Edit mode using the Esc or F10 key. After exiting, select the Compile option to compile the program. If any errors are detected, Turbo Prolog returns automatically to the Edit option, with the cursor at the error and an error

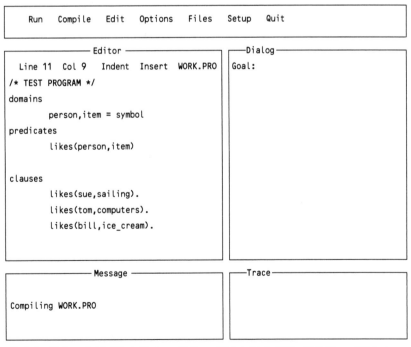

Figure 3.1
Editing a program

message at the bottom of the edit window. Correct the error, exit by pressing Esc or F10, and Turbo Prolog will compile again automatically.

After the program is compiled, select the Run option to initiate program execution. Use the Esc key to exit Run mode.

Editing Programs

Programs in the work area can be edited using the standard WordStar editing commands, shown in table 3.1. If you are familiar with Word-Star, you will have no problems editing with Turbo Prolog. The Esc or F10 key is always used to exit the editor.

Table 3.1
Turbo Prolog Editing Commands

Function	Command
Cursor Movement	
Character left	← or Ctrl-S
Character right	→ or Ctrl-D
Word left	Ctrl-← or Ctrl-A
Word right	Ctrl-→ or Ctrl-F
Line up	↑ or Ctrl-E
Line down	↓ or Ctrl-X
Page up	PgUp or Ctrl-R
Page down	PgDn or Ctrl-C
Beginning of line	Home or Ctrl-QS
End of line	End or Ctrl-QD
Top of file	Ctrl-PgUp or Ctrl-QR
End of file	Ctrl-PgDn or Ctrl-QC
Beginning of block	Ctrl-QB
End of block	Ctrl-QK
Insert/Delete	
Insert mode toggle	Ins or Ctrl-V
Delete left character	Backspace
Delete character under cursor	Del
Delete right word	Alt-→
Delete line	Ctrl-Y
Delete to end of line	Ctrl-QY
Block Commands	
Mark block begin	Ctrl-KB
Mark block end	Ctrl-KK
Copy block	F5 or Ctrl-KC
Move block	F6 or Ctrl-KV
Delete block	F7 or Ctrl-KY
Read block from disk	F9 or Ctrl-KR
Hide/display block	Ctrl-KH

Table 3.1 (cont.)

Function	Command
Miscellaneous	
Call auxiliary editor	F8
Go to line	F2
End edit	Esc or F10
Auto indent toggle	Ctrl-QI
Find	F3 or Ctrl-QF
Repeat last find	Ctrl-L
Find and replace	F4 or Ctrl-QA

Changing the Default Windows

For most of the examples in this book, you will probably find Turbo Prolog's default windows inadequate. You will probably want wider editor and dialog windows and you may want smaller trace and message windows.

To change the windows, use the Setup option in the menu. On the next displayed option window, select the Window Size option. Use the menu at the bottom of the screen and the arrow keys to resize the window. The Window Size menu permits you to change the size and position of any of the four windows. You can set both the dialog and editor windows to full screen width. When Prolog is in use, the active window at any time will overlay the other windows. After you have finished resizing the windows, save your new configuration using the same Setup option and Save configuration option.

Compiling Standalone Programs

In default mode, programs are compiled to execute internal to Turbo Prolog. The program is compiled to an executable form very quickly, and then executes under control of Turbo Prolog. This results in very fast development. You can move from editing to execution quickly, and then return to the editor, if necessary, just as quickly. Turbo Prolog, the editor, and your program are all in memory at the same time.

After the program is developed, however, this is a disadvantage. For internal execution, the user must have Turbo Prolog; also, each time the program is run, Turbo Prolog must be loaded with the program and the program must be compiled.

You can also compile programs to execute external to Turbo Prolog. To compile for external execution, use the Options menu. You can select to compile to an EXE or OBJ file. For your early experiments with external execution, select the EXE option. This is useful if you want to create and market an expert system. The user does not need Turbo

Prolog to run the program, and your source code is protected and cannot be seen by the user. Now let's see what this compile process does.

Preparing a source program to run as a standalone program (external execution) is a two-step process. In the first step, the compiler creates an OBJ file. Then, a linker must be used to convert the OBJ file to an executable EXE file. For example, if the source program TEST.PRO is compiled for external execution, Turbo Prolog would produce a TEST.OBJ file. A linker then converts this to a TEST.EXE file, which is executable without Turbo Prolog. If you select the EXE option, Turbo Prolog on compiling initiates the complete process: compile, link, and execute. On exiting Turbo Prolog, you will find the TEST.EXE file on the disk. You can then execute your program again by entering TEST without using Turbo Prolog.

> **Note:** Actually, after compiling, Turbo Prolog immediately exits to DOS. It then tries to execute your new program using the new EXE file. After execution, control is returned to Turbo Prolog. Both Turbo Prolog and your new program (as an EXE file) are in memory at the same time, permitting you to easily edit the program again and try another compilation. There are two disadvantages: the link process is somewhat time consuming (it takes a few minutes) and you will need a lot of computer memory to keep the source code, Turbo Prolog, and the compiled version all in memory. If the computer runs out of memory, your program will still compile but you will not be able to execute the program until you exit Turbo Prolog and run the program completely outside Turbo Prolog.

The OBJ option is used if you want to link your Prolog program with other modules created with other languages. Almost all compilers (for example, Pascal, BASIC, FORTRAN, and COBOL) produce OBJ files when compiling. You can create all the OBJ files you need for an application using any number of languages, then link these to the final system product with the linker.

Exercise

If you did not do so already, enter a short Turbo Prolog program, compile it, and then execute it. Use any early exercise in the Turbo Prolog manual.

chapter 4

The Prolog Language

□ To start a Prolog program execution, the user specifies a *goal,* which is a question about an object. For example, you might express as a goal:

```
diagnosed(starter_motor,true)
```

Prolog then attempts to prove that the goal is true by matching it against rules or facts that are in the program. After a Prolog program execution has been initiated by specifying a goal, there are three possible results:

- The goal succeeds; that is, it is proven true.
- The goal fails; that is, Prolog cannot match the goal with any fact or rule in the program.
- The program fails because of some error in the program.

Expressing Facts

Prolog permits you to express symbolic relationships as facts. For example, if Melody likes Bob, this can be expressed in Prolog as:

```
likes(melody,bob).
```

In this example, Melody and Bob are *objects*. The name of a symbolic object always begins with a lowercase letter.

The word *likes* is the name of a *relation*. A relation defines the manner in which objects belong together. The name of the relation also begins with a lowercase letter. Note the period at the end of the expression. The entire expression is called a *predicate*. A predicate is a function with a value of true or false. It expresses a property or a relationship.

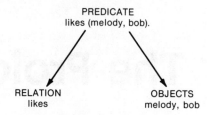

Figure 4.1
The predicate components

Components of other languages can be roughly compared with components of Prolog. The predicate is the function, the relation is the operator, and the objects are the arguments for the operator.

Because the operator is specified first, Prolog would be described as using prefix notation. Some Prolog arithmetical expressions may use infix notation.

In some cases, the predicate may not have an argument. If there is no argument, the predicate always evaluates as true:

```
defective_starter_motor.
```

We could continue to add other facts to our system:

```
likes(melody,bob).
likes(melody,skiing).
likes(tom,reading).
likes(jane,bob).
```

After these facts are stored in our system, a goal for the system could be defined:

```
likes(tom,reading)
```

The program then tries to match this goal with the facts in the program. If the search is successful (as in this case), the program returns:

```
True
```

Now suppose we enter as a goal:

```
likes(melody,tom)
```

In this case, the program can find no match and returns the answer:

```
False
```

This does not mean necessarily that Melody does not like Tom; it just means the program does not have enough information to make the decision. In an expert system, *False* indicates a failure to make a match with the current information, not that the goal is necessarily untrue. If you want to express that a fact is not true, you must use the *not* predicate (discussed later in this chapter).

In a program, the expression:

```
likes(melody,bob).
```

may mean Melody likes Bob or that Bob likes Melody. Prolog is quite indifferent to the interpretation (what the user has assigned to the meaning of *likes*). You could use *likes* to refer to either type of relation in a program, but you should be consistent within a given program.

Prolog Objects

We can use any number of objects in stating a fact (i.e., a predicate can have any number of arguments). Following are some symbolic expressions and their corresponding facts in English:

`is(jack,vegetarian).`	Jack is a vegetarian.
`likes(bill,computers).`	Bill likes computers.
`has(cat,black_tail).`	The cat has a black tail.
`diagnosis(defective,starter_motor).`	The diagnosis is a defective starter motor.
`diagnosis(starter_motor,true).`	The diagnosis is a defective starter motor.
`diagnosis(starter_motor).`	The diagnosis is a defective starter motor.
`car(blue,3000,1981,pontiac).`	The car is a blue, $3000, 1981 Pontiac.
`location(bill,home).`	Bill is at home.
`age(tom,12).`	Tom is twelve years old.

Notice several things about these Prolog statements:

1. An object symbol may represent a physical entity or an abstract concept. It can be a noun or an adjective. Following are some examples of object symbols:

```
cat
bob
blue
12
true
```

Note: In part 2, you will be introduced to the basic concepts of representing knowledge. In the theory of knowledge representation, symbols represent real objects. These representative objects have properties or attributes, and attributes have values. A car is an object, color is an attribute, and blue is a value. The Turbo Prolog manual uses the concept of object to apply to any simple predicate argument whether it is a true object (physical or conceptual), property, or value. In part 1, the term *object* refers to the Prolog language object, which is really a simple argument term.

2. You may have any number of object symbols for a given relation.

3. The name of each object symbol begins with a lowercase letter and contains letters, digits, or an underscore.

4. All the words of the equivalent English sentence are not necessarily in the Prolog fact. The Prolog relation has an implied meaning that is consistent in a given program. There are many ways of expressing a particular fact, but it is important to use a consistent representation in a given program.

5. Symbolic objects are always singular. In the expression *Bill likes computers, computers* is a singular object.

6. You can define your own order for the arguments, but after this order is defined it should remain consistent within the program.

Objects are roughly equivalent to the constants in procedural programming. With Prolog, however, the object is a much more powerful concept. Symbolic objects represent real-world entities, concepts, properties of entities, properties of concepts, or values.

In naming an object, you may use any number of characters. The name must start with a lowercase letter, but except for the first letter you can use uppercase letters, lowercase letters, numbers, or underscore characters. For most types of object names, you should avoid using commas, asterisks, and operator symbols (for example, + and −) in the name. Certain names are reserved by Turbo Prolog and should not be used in a program. See table 4.1.

The Turbo Prolog Program

The Turbo Prolog program consists of three essential sections: *domains, predicates,* and *clauses.* In some applications, you will want

Table 4.1
Reserved Names in Turbo Prolog

abs	dir	left	reference
and	disk	length	removewindow
arctan	display	line	renamefile
asserta	div	ln	retract
assertz	domains	log	right
attribute	dot	makewindow	round
back	edit	membyte	save
beep	editmsg	memword	scr__attr
bios	eof	mod	scr__char
bitand	existfile	nl	scroll
bitleft	exit	nobreak	shiftwindow
bitnot	exp	not	shorttrace
bitor	fail	nowarnings	sin
bitright	field__attr	openappend	sound
bitxor	filemode	openmodify	sqrt
bound	filepos	openread	storage
char__int	file__str	openwrite	str__char
check__determ	findall	or	str__int
clauses	flush	pencolor	str__len
clearwindow	forward	pendown	str__real
closefile	free	penpos	system
code	frontchar	penup	tan
comline	frontstr	port__byte	text
concat	fronttoken	predicates	time
consult	global	project	trace
cos	goal	ptr__dword	trail
cursor	gotowindow	random	upper__lower
cursorform	if	readchar	window__attr
database	include	readdevice	window__str
date	inkey	readint	write
deletefile	isname	readln	write__device
diagnostics	keypressed	readreal	writef

to add additional sections, such as *database* or *goal*. Each section must be identified with a keyword and the sequence of these sections is important. An example showing these basic sections is shown in listing 4.1.

Listing 4.1
A sample Prolog program

```
/* SAMPLE PROLOG PROGRAM  */

domains
  item,part=symbol

predicates
  has(item,part)
```

Listing 4.1 (cont.)

```
clauses
  has(car,alternator).
  has(car,battery).
  has(car,voltage_regulator).
  has(car,starter_motor).
  has(alternator,brushes).
  has(starter_motor,relay).
```

The *clauses* section contains all the facts, and the rules that express any relationships between these facts. Any procedural control is also in the clauses section—for example, when Prolog attempts to prove a goal, program execution starts at the first clause.

The *predicates* section defines the objects in each clause. Each relation name in each clause must have a corresponding definition in the predicates section. The predicate does not end with a period. For example, we might have the following expression in the clauses section:

```
is(starter_motor,defective).
```

In the predicates section, we need to have the following predicate:

```
is(part,status)
```

You can have multiple predicates for the same relation in the predicates section:

```
is(item,part,status)
is(part,status)
```

This permits you to use different types of variables at different times with the same relation. Then, each predicate behaves as a separate predicate. As far as Prolog is concerned, these are two predicates with nothing in common. Prolog sees no common relation or argument, even though the two *is, part,* and *status* names are the same.

The *domains* section "types" the objects, specifying the types of values that can be used for the objects that are part of each predicate. Most languages have some typing control. This enables the program to set up the proper storage for values and permits better control over execution. For example, the character string *WISDOM* is stored quite differently from the number *12.324,* which again is stored differently from the integer number *1234.*

It is the same in a Prolog program. There must be some way of allocating computer storage for the objects if the program is to run most efficiently. This is the function of the domains section. Each object in the predicates section must have a corresponding domain defined in the domains section.

Types of Objects

There are six types of domains that are available to the Turbo Prolog programmer: char, integer, real, string, symbol, and file. Refer to table 4.2. For example, the expression:

```
is(starter_motor,defective).
```

translates to: *The starter motor is defective.* We have the predicate:

```
is(part,status)
```

and the corresponding statement in the domains section:

```
part,status = symbol
```

> **Note:** It is technically possible to omit the domains section in some programs by defining object types in the predicates section. For example, if the predicate was:
>
> ```
> is(symbol,symbol)
> ```
>
> the program would still function, and a domains section would not be needed to specify any domain types for this predicate.

Table 4.2
Turbo Prolog Domain Types

Domain Type	Meaning
char	single character (enclosed between single quotation marks)
integer	integers from $-32,768$ to $32,767$
real	floating point numbers ($1e^{-307}$ to $1e^{308}$)
string	character sequence (enclosed between double quotation marks)
symbol	any character sequence of letters, numbers, and underscores, with the first character in lowercase
file	symbolic file name

The type of domain used for a particular object depends upon how the object is used in the program. The different types are stored differently internal to the program. For example, if *starter_motor* is an object that is used internally and never displayed on the screen, it would be proper to use it as a symbolic type as *starter_motor*. If it will be displayed on the screen with a space as "starter motor," you would want it to be a string type, but you will have to use double quotation marks in the program wherever the object is used. With names and addresses that will be displayed with a mixture of uppercase and lower-case with embedded commas and other punctuation, the string type is most appropriate (such as "John Smith" or "3207 Capital, Suite 407").

Ordering the Clauses

Even though Prolog is not considered a procedural language, there is an implied procedural control. For each predicate in the predicates section, there may be two or more clauses in the clauses section. The order of the clauses for each predicate is important.

In a specific program, the order of the clauses may be important for two reasons:

1. The order of the clauses for a particular predicate determines the efficiency of the program. Prolog program execution is a matching process and also a linear process in an IBM PC compatible machine. Prolog tries to resolve the goal starting at the first clause of the first predicate in the program matching the specified goal.

2. In using special program features such as recursion and the cut (explained in chapters 8 and 10), the order of the clauses for a particular predicate controls the flow of program execution. Reordering the clauses makes the program run differently.

You can create definite procedures that control a program's execution by using special predicates (explained in chapter 8), by controlling the order of the components of the antecedent of a rule (see chapter 5), and by controlling the order of the clauses for a predicate.

Using Variables

At this point in our study of Prolog, we have only verified goals using facts that were previously stored. This is certainly not too exciting, but let us see what happens when we add variable capability to our programs.

Our sample Prolog program (refer back to listing 4.1) includes a list of facts about a car. We could specify as a goal:

```
has(car,alternator)
```

and it would return the value of:

```
True
```

You could also ask a lot of questions about other parts, getting a true or false answer each time. Suppose, however, that you want a list of

all the parts in the car as defined by the facts. You could do this by
entering as a goal:

```
has(car,Part)
```

The word *Part* in this example is a *variable*. Variables always begin with
an uppercase letter. The remaining letters in the name can be uppercase
or lowercase.

If you try this example, you will see that Turbo Prolog displays a
list of all parts for the object *car:*

```
Part=battery
Part=alternator
Part=voltage_regulator
Part=starter_motor
```

Now let's look at what really happens when you enter this goal.
When the goal is specified, program execution starts. The goal with its
variable *Part* becomes a template. Turbo Prolog tries to match the
template, beginning with the first matching predicate. Each clause that
matches the template is listed as a solution of the goal.

Compound Goals

We can also use variables in the same way to specify compound goals:

```
has(car,Part) and has(Part,Component)
```

This goal has two variables, *Part* and *Component*. When this goal is
specified, Turbo Prolog begins by using the first condition as a template,
trying to find a matching fact starting at the first clause. Because the first
clause matches, the value of *Part* is said to be *bound* to *battery.* Prolog
also sets an internal pointer, remembering where it was when trying for a
match on the first part.

Prolog then creates a new template using the second condition:

```
has(battery,Component)
```

and begins to search for a match from the beginning of the clauses. The
search fails; so the second part of the goal fails and Turbo Prolog again
returns to the first part of the goal. The variable *Part* is free again and
Prolog attempts a match, continuing from its position when solving the
first part of the goal by using the pointer. This time the value of *Part* is
set to *alternator.* A new template is created:

```
has(alternator,Component)
```

The pointer is set so Prolog can remember where it was, and another attempt is made to solve the second part of the goal using this as a template. A match will be found this time, with *Component* bound to *brushes*. The goal has been satisfied with the values.

Prolog still does not quit. It continues to search for other matches of the compound goal, but it will find no others. After completion, Turbo Prolog displays the resulting matches with the value *True* to indicate that the goal was satisfied at least once:

```
Part=alternator    Component=brushes
True
```

A goal that consists of at least two subgoals, as in this example, is a compound goal. We can use any logical and relational operators (see table 4.3) in defining the compound goal. For example, the following are acceptable compound goals:

```
car(Color,Price,Year,Make) and Price<3000
letter(X) or X<= 'a'
```

Notice that *Color, Price, Year, Make, and X* are all variables in this example.

Table 4.3
Turbo Prolog Relational Operators

Operator	Meaning
<	less than
<=	less than or equal to
=	equal
>	greater than
>=	greater than or equal to
><	different from (not equal to)

If a particular object in a predicate is of no importance in the solution of the goal, the variable can be replaced with an underscore in defining the goal:

```
has(car,Part) and has(Part,_)
```

This would list all parts that had components. There would be two in this example.

Free and Bound Variables

At any given time, a variable may be said to be free or bound. A *free variable* is one that does not currently have any value. A *bound variable*, in contrast, has a fixed value.

In the previous example, *Part* and *Component* start as free variables. As soon as the first part of the compound goal matches the first clause, *Part* is set equal to *voltage_regulator* and becomes a bound variable. The match for the second part of the goal fails. *Part* is now a free variable again and the search continues from the second clause. The next match is found and *Part* becomes a bound variable again with the value *alternator*. The second part of the goal is satisfied with *Component* matching *brushes*. *Component* is now a bound variable. For a goal to be satisfied, all specified variables must become bound.

The following rules apply to variable binding:

1. All variables have a name that starts with an uppercase letter.

2. Variable names are unique to a given clause. The same name in another clause is a different variable.

3. Variables, at a given time, are always either bound or free.

4. You cannot assign a value to a variable that is already bound (see next section).

5. The binding applies only to the specific clause invoked. Variables are not "passed" to other clauses. The matching process binds the variables in the next clause called (explained in chapter 5).

6. When a variable is bound, it is the same type as the value to which it is bound. If a variable is bound to the value of *3,* and *3* is an object declared in the domains section as an integer type, the variable behaves as an integer type. If *3* is defined as a real type, the variable behaves as a real type. After the variable is bound, it will only match an object of the same type and value.

7. Under certain conditions in the execution of a program, a variable may lose its binding and become free again. This involves the concept of backtracking, which is discussed in chapter 8.

The Equal Operator

The equal operator functions in a special way with Turbo Prolog programs. For example, assume the following fact:

```
X = 3.
```

If the variable *X* is not bound when the clause is invoked, the value of *X* will be bound to the value of *3* after the invocation. If the variable *X* is already bound when the clause is invoked, the clause will return the value of *True* if *X* is bound to *3,* and return the value of *False* if *X* is bound to any other value.

If you define a goal as:

```
X = Y
```

the goal will succeed if both variables are bound and they are bound to the same value. It will fail if they do not match. If X is free and Y is bound, the goal will succeed and X will be bound to the same object to which Y is bound. Objects are always equal to themselves. You cannot assign a value to a variable that already has an assigned value. As with all variables, a binding only exists for the single clause.

Note: Some Prolog implementations include an *is* predicate that is used with arithmetical operations in a way similar to Turbo Prolog's equal sign.

Using Standard Predicates

Prolog has many *built-in* or *standard* predicates. As we shall see in the next chapter, all Prolog program execution is primarily a matching process. Even arithmetical operations must use predicates. Turbo Prolog, like most implementations, includes built-in predicates for arithmetical operations (see chapter 10).

Most versions of Prolog also contain other built-in predicates that perform other useful operations, such as writing text to the screen and reading characters from the keyboard. Turbo Prolog contains more than ninety built-in predicates in addition to the arithmetical predicates. These can be used to convert object types, perform operations with character strings, manage dynamic databases, and do other useful functions. Many of these are useful in developing expert systems and will be introduced, as needed, in various chapter examples. Turbo Prolog's built-in predicates can be classified into nine groups. See table 4.4.

Table 4.4
Turbo Prolog's Built-In Predicates

Predicate	Function
Reading predicates	Predicates for reading data from the keyboard
Writing predicates	Predicates for writing data to the screen or a file
File management predicates	Predicates for managing disk files from a Prolog program
Screen handling predicates	Predicates for controlling the monitor and graphic displays
String handling predicates	Operational predicates for string data
Type conversion predicates	Predicates for converting data types
Data predicates	Predicates for managing dynamic databases (see chapter 7)
System level predicates	Predicates for interfacing a Prolog program to DOS
Language predicates	Special predicates for controlling Prolog execution

Using the Not Predicate

The *not* predicate is a standard (built-in) Turbo Prolog predicate that can be used to express that a goal is true if a fact is not true. For example:

```
ill(bob) :-
not(location(bob(work))).
```

Remember that if a fact is not in the database, Prolog considers it as *false*. False implies that knowledge is not available for making an adequate decision. If a fact is expressly not true (that is, it is really false), it must be defined as such using the *not* predicate.

Comments in Programs

It is a good idea to include comments in your Turbo Prolog programs to explain what is happening. You should at least include some type of title and you will probably want to add a date and other information.

You can add comments to any program by starting the comment with a /* and ending the comment with an */. For example:

```
/* AUTOMOBILE DIAGNOSTIC SYSTEM
        6/16/86                        */
```

The comment can be part of a line with other code or, as in the previous example, on separate lines. Use comments liberally in your coding to help document your work.

Exercises

1. Which of the following are valid object names? What is the type of each valid name?

    a. John

    b. "JOHN"

    c. "John"

    d. 'John'

    e. 12

    f. john

    g. a

    h. 'a'

    i. aBLE

    j. john smith

    k. beep

2. Which of the following are valid variable names?

    a. Type

    b. Beep

    c. TemPorary

    d. Address12

    e. First name

3. Identify whether each of the following is a variable or object name.

    a. name

    b. defective

    c. Cost

    d. product__cost

    e. Employee age

chapter | 5 |

Using Prolog Rules

☐ You can also create rules with Prolog. Rules permit you to infer new facts from existing facts. In this chapter, you will learn how to create Prolog rules and how to use them effectively.

The Rule

Sometimes you may want to express that the truth of a particular fact depends upon other facts. For example, you might want to say:

> IF the engine does not turn over
>
> AND the battery voltage is good
>
> AND the starter motor relay pulls in
>
> AND the starter motor does not turn with a grinding sound
>
> THEN the starter motor is defective.
>
> This could be expressed using Turbo Prolog as:

```
defective(starter_motor) if
  engine_turns_over(false) and
  battery_charged(true) and
  relay(true) and
  starter_motor(false).
```

Notice the general form of the Prolog rule. The goal (a hypothesis) is stated first, followed by the word *if*. The conditions upon which the goal depends are stated next, each connected by the word *and*. The rule, like a fact, is terminated with a period.

> **Note:** In this chapter and the next few chapters, an automotive diagnostic system is used as an expert system example. It is only a small and consistent set of rules to illustrate some Prolog principles. It is not a full expert system.

Each condition is placed on a separate line and indented from the conclusion. We do this simply to make the rule more readable; it is not a requirement for proper execution. The hypothesis and each condition look very much like predicate facts and each has a value of either true or false.

A rule is a statement about objects and their relationships. It permits us to deduce new facts from existing facts. Any Prolog program is a list of facts and rules. The rules and facts together are a *database*. Because rules are such an important part of Prolog programs, it is useful to develop a type of shorthand for expressing a rule. We can express the rule of the previous example in an abbreviated form as:

```
defective(starter_motor) :-
  engine_turns_over(false),
  battery_charged(true),
  relay(true),
  starter_motor(false).
```

The :- is called a break and indicates *if*. A comma represents the *and*.

The process of using such rules to solve a problem is called *formal reasoning, inference,* or *deduction*. Sherlock Holmes used deduction to solve crimes in nineteenth century England. We all use the process of deduction every day: when the car doesn't start, when a family member leaves the cap off the toothpaste, when we try to guess the weather for a golf game on Saturday, or when a young man tries to decide when and how to ask a girl for a date. In each case, you are trying to deduce new facts from existing facts.

The only logical connective permitted in a rule is the *and*. If you need to relate the success of a hypothesis to either of two or more factual relationships (the *or* connective), you use multiple rules:

```
defective(starter_motor) :-
  engine_turns_over(false),
  battery_charged(true),
  relay(true),
  starter_motor(false).

defective(starter_motor) :-
  starter_motor(true).
```

We can now express as our goal:

```
defective(starter_motor)
```

and Prolog will begin by trying to prove the first rule. If this fails, Prolog will try to prove the second rule.

Rule Components

Each rule consists of a *head* and a *body*. The head is the hypothesis and represents the goal we are trying to prove. In the previous example, the head of the first rule is:

```
defective(starter_motor)
```

The body is the remainder of the rule and is a compound subgoal consisting of several conditions. Each of the conditions in the body must be satisfied for the head (goal) to be true.

Variables in Rules

You can also use variables in rules by making general statements about relationships. For example:

```
sister(Person1,Person2) :-
  female(Person1),
  parents(Person1,Mother,Father),
  parents(Person2,Mother,Father).
```

This states that *Person1* is the sister of *Person2* if *Person1* is female and both share the same parents. Notice that variables that are part of the body do not need to be part of the head.

You can also use variables in a goal. For example, suppose we define a goal as:

```
defective(X)
```

Prolog begins by trying to find the first hypothesis (conclusion) that matches the goal (and binding X), then tries to prove that each condition in the premise is true. If any condition fails, Prolog searches for the next hypothesis that matches the goal, binds X again, and tries to prove the premise true.

Using Rules

Now let's see how we can use rules to prove a particular goal (new fact) from facts that are already in the database. Suppose, for example, you have the following (try substituting your family members in this):

```
              sister(Person1,Person2) :-
                female(Person1),
                parents(Person1,Mother,Father),
                parents(Person2,Mother,Father).

            male(carl).
            male(herman).
            male(paul).
            male(tim).
            male(luke).

            female(sandy).
            female(gertrude).
            female(carol).
            female(edna).
            female(grace).

            parents(sandy,gertrude,herman).
            parents(luke,grace,paul).
            parents(edna,gertrude,herman).
```

Now try as a goal:

```
sister(sandy,edna)
```

When execution begins, the following happens.

1. The variables *Person1* and *Person2* begin as free variables.

2. Prolog searches for the head of a rule matching the goal:

```
    sister(Person1,Person2)
```

binding the value of *Person1* in the predicate to *sandy* and the value of *Person2* to *edna*.

3. Prolog now accepts the head of the rule as a hypothesis and tries to solve each premise of the body.

4. The first condition is *female(sandy)* because *Person1* is bound to *sandy*. This becomes a new goal and this goal succeeds. Prolog marks this place in the clause because it must return to this point and try to find another path if any condition fails beyond this point. Both variables remain bound.

5. Prolog now tries to satisfy the goal:

```
    parents(sandy,Mother,Father)
```

The variables *Mother* and *Father* are free variables.

6. The goal is satisfied with the fact:

```
parents(sandy,gertrude,herman).
```

Mother is bound to *gertrude,* and *Father* to *herman.* Prolog marks this place in case further subgoals fail and you must return here.

7. The final subgoal contains only bound variables:

```
parents(edna,gertrude,herman).
```

This will succeed, so the entire rule succeeds. The hypothesis is proved true, so our original goal is true. Prolog answers *True.*

Using Goals with Variables

Now suppose we take this same example and specify as a goal:

```
sister(edna,Person2)
```

In this case, the goal matches the first rule. *Person1* becomes bound to *edna* and *Person2* remains free for the moment. Then the following takes place.

1. The first subgoal is:

```
female(edna)
```

This is found true, and the place is marked.

2. The second subgoal becomes:

```
parents(edna,Mother,Father)
```

The first matching fact is found and *Mother* becomes bound to *gertrude,* and *Father* becomes bound to *herman.* The place is marked. If subgoals fail further down, we must return here and try to find another match (there would be none). In this example, however, the subgoal succeeded.

3. The next goal is:

```
parents(Person2,gertrude,herman)
```

This matches the fact:

```
parents(sandy,gertrude,herman).
```

binding *Person2* to *sandy.*

4. Because all subgoals succeed, the hypothesis is proven true with *Person2* bound to *sandy.* Turbo Prolog prints:

```
Person2=sandy
True
```

Notice that there may be other solutions (for example, if *sandy* had two sisters). In designing an expert system, you must decide whether you want all solutions displayed or only the first displayed. If you are designing a medical diagnostic system, for example, you would want to display all solutions (diseases) that relate to specific symptoms.

Using Backtracking to Prove Goals

Now let's see how we can use rules to prove a goal in our simple expert system. Listing 5.1 is a Turbo Prolog listing of a simple expert system.

Listing 5.1
Automotive diagnostic system (simple system)

```
/*      AUTOMOTIVE DIAGNOSTIC SYSTEM
             (SIMPLE SYSTEM)

   Type RUN in response to the GOAL prompt at runtime. */

predicates

   run
   diagnosed(symbol)
   battery_connections(symbol)
   battery_charged(symbol)
   battery_water(symbol)
   starter_motor(symbol)
   relay(symbol)
   engine_turns_over(symbol)
   spark(symbol)

clauses

   run:-
      diagnosed(X),!,
      write("Check ",X),nl.

   run:-
      write("\nUnable to determine what"),
      write(" your problem is. \n").

   /* Set this parameter false if the battery's water
      level is low. */
   battery_water(true).
```

Listing 5.1 (cont.)

```
/* Set this parameter false if battery connections are
   poor. */
battery_connections(true).

/* Set this parameter false if headlights are dim. */
battery_charged(false).
/* Set this parameter false if starter motor turns
   with a grinding sound. */
starter_motor(true).

/* Set this parameter false if starter motor relay
   does not pull in, even if the starter motor does
   not turn over. */
relay(true).

/* Set this parameter false if motor does not turn
   over. */
engine_turns_over(false).

/* Set this parameter false if plug or distributor
   connections are bad. */
spark(true).

diagnosed(starter_motor) if
  engine_turns_over(false) and
  battery_charged(true) and
  relay(true) and
  starter_motor(false).

diagnosed(battery_connections) if
  engine_turns_over(false) and
  battery_charged(true) and
  battery_connections(false).

diagnosed(battery_water) if
  engine_turns_over(false) and
  battery_charged(true) and
  battery_connections(true),
  battery_water(false).

diagnosed(battery_charged) if
  engine_turns_over(false) and
  battery_charged(false) and
  battery_connections(true),
  battery_water(true),
  battery_charged(false).
```

51

Listing 5.1 (cont.)

```
diagnosed(fuse) if
    engine_turns_over(false) and
    battery_charged(true) and
    relay(false).

diagnosed(spark_plugs) if
    engine_turns_over(true) and
    spark(false).

diagnosed(fuel) if
    engine_turns_over(true) and
    spark(true).
```

Facts we know about the problem are stated as clauses at the beginning of the program. To start the program, we specify as the goal:

```
diagnosed(X)
```

Prolog tries to match this with a fact or the head of a rule in the clauses section. It finds a match on the first clause:

```
diagnosed(starter_motor) :-
    engine_turns_over(false) and
    battery_charged(true) and
    relay(true) and
    starter_motor(false).
```

Prolog then tries to prove this true. To do this, each of the subgoals must be found as true. Prolog marks this place in the clauses section, then assumes a new goal as:

```
engine_turns_over(false)
```

This matches a fact clause at the beginning (true), so the testing continues. The first condition that will fail is *battery_charged(true)*. After this fails, the goal *diagnosed(starter_motor)* fails.

Prolog then backtracks to the initial goal, trying to find another match for *diagnosed(X)*. Each rule will fail, in turn, until the program reaches:

```
diagnosed(battery_charged)
```

Prolog now tries to prove this hypothesis. This time the goal succeeds, resulting in the goal *run* succeeding.

> **Note:** The exclamation point in the *run* clause prevents the execution of the second *run* clause. This is discussed in chapter 8.

Prolog program execution, then, is a pattern-matching process of moving through a hierarchy of goals. To prove the original goal, Prolog tries to find a matching fact or rule hypothesis. If it is a rule, Prolog marks the place and tries to prove each of the subgoals in the body of the rule. Each condition in the body becomes a goal in turn, and Prolog tries to prove each of these. As soon as any of the conditions in the body fail, Prolog backtracks and tries to find another predicate matching the original goal. This continues until all predicates matching the original goal are checked.

The execution becomes a relentless search through the rules, moving downward through successive goals until each succeeds or fails. On a failure, the program backtracks, trying to follow another route and find another matching hypothesis or fact for the original goal.

Unification

The process by which Prolog tries to match a subgoal against facts and the heads of other rules to prove the subgoal is called *unification*. It is a pattern-matching operation and the essential technique that Prolog uses to solve the original goal.

A simple term is said to unify with another term if they both have the same predicate, the same number of arguments, the arguments are of the same domain type, and all of the subterms unify with each other. If a free variable is unified with another term, the free variable will be bound to the values of that term. For example:

```
diagnosed(X)
```

unifies with:

```
diagnosed(starter_motor)
```

binding *X* to *starter_motor*.

Unification functions much like parameter passing in procedural programming and can even do certain tests for equality or comparison. A summary of the unification rules follows.

1. A free variable will unify with any term. As a result, the variable is bound to the term.
2. A constant can unify with itself or any free variable.
3. A variable can unify with any variable. After unifying, the two variables act as one.

Controlling the Search

Although Prolog is not considered a procedural language, the order of the clauses is important for efficient operation of the program. In part 2, you will learn more about how to define and order the rules, but for now let's look at how the Prolog language interprets a given clause order. The basic rules follow.

1. All clauses for the same predicate must be grouped together in the program. In our diagnostic program, for example, all *diagnostic(X)* predicates are grouped together.

2. Predicate clauses for the same predicate are tested in the order in which they appear in the program. In the example, the first predicate tested for the goal *diagnosed(X)* is:

```
diagnosed(starter_motor)
```

3. In a rule, the head becomes the goal and the body is composed of one or more subgoals. These subgoals are tested in the order in which they appear in the rule. For:

```
diagnosed(starter_motor)
```

the first subgoal tested is:

```
engine_turns_over(false)
```

4. In a rule, the goal (conclusion) is satisfied only if all subgoals (conditions) succeed. If any subgoal fails, the goal fails and further subgoals in the rule are not tested.

Exercises

1. Using Turbo Prolog, enter listing 5.1. Because the program will be used with other exercises, save it as file AUTO1.PRO. Execute the program, specifying a goal of *diagnosed(X)*. Does the goal succeed? If so, with what value of *X?*

2. Edit the original program so that the first *diagnosed(X)* clause begins:

```
diagnosed(starter-motor) :-
    trace(on),
    engine_turns_over(false).
```

Add the word *trace* as the first word in listing 5.1. Start the execution using *diagnosed(X)* as the goal again, and use the F10 key to go through each step in turn. Monitor the path of the execution process, writing each goal in turn that Prolog tries to prove.

chapter 6

The User Interface— Simple Input and Output

☐ In the automobile diagnostic system built in the last chapter, the facts that were known about the problem were stated at the beginning of the program. This input method has several disadvantages:

- A large number of facts must be defined, many of which are not relevant to the problem.
- The program must be recompiled each time we are faced with a new problem and the facts are different.
- There is no interaction (consultation) with the user during program execution.

What is needed is some way to direct questions to the user and define facts from the user's answers during program execution. Questions to the user need to be in English, using a vocabulary that the user can understand. In this chapter, you will learn some simple techniques to improve the user interface.

Output

The *write* predicate is the standard predicate for outputting any object or variable of a standard domain type.

The Write Predicate

Listing 6.1 is a new form of our program using input and output statements.

Listing 6.1
Automotive diagnostic system with input and output

```
/*      AUTOMOTIVE DIAGNOSTIC SYSTEM
            with input and output

    Type RUN in response to the GOAL prompt at runtime. */

predicates

    run
    diagnosed(symbol)
    check(symbol)
    response(char)

clauses

    run:-
      write("AUTOMOBILE DIAGNOSTIC SYSTEM"),nl,
      diagnosed(_),!,nl.

    run:-
      write("\nUnable to determine what"),
      write(" your problem is. \n").

    diagnosed(starter_motor) :-
      not(check(engine_turns_over)),
      check(electrical_power),
      check(relay),
      not(check(starter_motor)),
      write("Replace starter motor"),nl.

    diagnosed(battery_connections) :-
      not(check(engine_turns_over)),
      not(check(electrical_power)),
      not(check(battery_connections)),
      write("Tighten battery connections."),nl.

    diagnosed(battery_water) :-
      not(check(engine_turns_over)),
      not(check(electrical_power)),
      check(battery_connections),
      not(check(battery_water)),
      write("Fill battery with water."),nl.
```

Listing 6.1 (cont.)

```
diagnosed(battery_charged) :-
  not(check(engine_turns_over)),
  not(check(electrical_power)),
  check(battery_connections),
  check(battery_water),
  not(check(battery_charged)),
  write("Battery is not charged. Try jumping it to
    start"),nl,
  write("then check for loose or broken fan belt or
    defective"),nl,
  write("regulator."),nl.

diagnosed(relay) :-
  not(check(engine_turns_over)),
  check(electrical_power),
  not(check(relay)),
  write("Check ignition fuse, key switch, and
    starter motor"),nl,
  write("relay."),nl.

diagnosed(spark_delivery_system) :-
  check(engine_turns_over),
  not(check(spark_delivery_system)),
  write("Check distributor, spark plugs, and related
    wiring."),nl.

 diagnosed(fuel_system) :-
  check(engine_turns_over),
  check(spark_delivery_system),
  write("Check gas gauge, fuel filter, and
    'possibility of"),nl,
  write("flooding."),nl.

check(battery_connections) :-
  write("Are the battery connections good (y/n)? "),
  response(Reply),Reply='n'.

check(electrical_power) :-
  write("Are the headlights dim or do they fail to
    light "),nl,
  write("when turned on (y/n)? "),nl,
  response(Reply),Reply='n'.

check(battery_water) :-
  write("Is the battery water level good (y/n)? "),nl,
  response(Reply),Reply='y'.

check(engine_turns_over) :-
```

Listing 6.1 (cont.)

```
write("Does the engine turn over normally without
  starting (y/n) ? "),nl,
response(Reply),
Reply='y'.

check(spark_delivery_system) :-
write("Are the spark plug and distributor wires
  good (y/n)? "),nl,
response(Reply),
Reply='y'.

check(starter_motor) :-
write("Does the starter motor fail to turn, turn
  slowly,"),nl,
write("or turn with an abnormal grinding sound
  (y/n)? "),nl,
response(Reply),
Reply='n'.

check(relay) :-
write("Can you hear the starter motor relay"),nl,
write("pull in (y/n)? "),nl,
response(Reply),
Reply='y'.

check(battery_charged) :-
write("Is the battery fully charged
  (y/n) ? "),nl,
response(Reply),
Reply='y'.

response(Reply) :-
readchar(Reply),
write(Reply),nl.
```

To start this program, it is only necessary to enter *run* when Prolog prompts for a goal. This will then match the following clause:

```
run :-
  diagnosed(X),
  write("Replace ",X),nl.
```

Our primary interest at this point is the last line of the rule. The *write* predicate is a standard (or built-in) predicate; that is, it is an internal part of Turbo Prolog and does not need to be defined by the user or made part of the predicates section. The general form of the predicate is:

```
write(X1,X1,X3,...Xn)
```

where *Xn* represents an object or bound variable. In the example, if *X* is bound to *starter__motor,* execution of the predicate would display:

```
Replace starter_motor
```

The variables can be any of the standard domain types: symbol, character, integer, or real.

When an output predicate is encountered in a rule, it evaluates as *True* and is executed immediately. This is similar to any other type of sequential programming, with the execution proceeding left to right and top to bottom:

```
write("Unable to determine what "),
write("your problem is.").
```

displays as:

```
Unable to determine what your problem is.
```

You can also use multiple variables in an output predicate. For example:

```
check(grind,starter_motor).

query:-
  check(X,Y),
  write("Does the ",Y," ",X," ? ").
```

Output Control

If an object name begins with a backslash and is of a character or string domain, it is considered a special control character. The following control characters are valid:

\t   Tabulate

\n   New line (carriage return)

\b   Backslash

For example, the following are all identical:

```
write("\n")
write('\n')
```

You can also use the *nl* standard predicate to indicate a new line function. For example:

```
write("Does the starter motor turn with an"),nl,
write("abnormal grinding sound?"),nl.
```

or:

```
write("Does the starter motor turn with an\n"),
write("abnormal grinding sound?\n").
```

would display as:

```
Does the starter motor turn with an
abnormal grinding sound?
```

Formatted Output

You can use the *writef* standard predicate to display formatted output. This permits you to align decimals and justify strings. The standard form of the *writef* predicate is:

```
writef(format,X1,X2,X3,...Xn)
```

where *format* is defined as *%-m.p* as follows:

%   Delimiter indicating format will follow

–   Denotes left justification; default is right justification

m   Optional parameter that indicates minimum field width

p   Optional parameter that indicates precision of floating point number or maximum string characters

The *p* parameter can also include the letter *f, e,* or *g* to indicate the type of numeric format:

f   Fixed point (default)

e   Exponential

g   General (use whatever is shortest)

When using the formatted *write* predicate, all output argument values are printed with the same format. If you need to print values with different formats, use multiple format predicates.

Outputting Common Text Strings

There may be times when you want to use a common output string in several rules. For example, the text string:

```
Replace power supply.
```

may be a conclusion of several rules. If you want to conserve computer memory and use a common text string, set up a separate predicate to bind the text string to a variable, then output the variable:

```
diagnosed(power_supply) :-
  check(power_supply),
```

```
  outbind(power_supply,Power),
  write(Power),nl.

outbind(power_supply,X) :-
  X = "Replace power supply."
```

The *outbind(power_supply,X)* predicate can be used with many rules and the text string is only stored once in the program.

If several clauses share the same output, you can also use a separate predicate for outputting:

```
diagnosed(power_supply) :-
  check(power_supply),
  cause(power_supply).

cause(power_supply) :-
  write("Power supply is defective."),nl,
  write("Replace power supply."),nl.
```

Input

For an interactive dialog with the user, you also need to be able to get answers from the user and use these answers to define facts. This can be implemented with the proper type of *read* standard predicate.

The Read Predicates

One way to do this is to use the *readln* standard predicate. This permits the user to read in any character string. For example:

```
check(starter_motor):-
  write("Does the starter motor have a ",),nl,
  write("grinding sound (yes/no) ?"),nl,
  readln(Reply),
  Reply="yes".
```

After the question is asked, program execution will pause and wait for the user to enter the answer. The answer must be entered in lowercase and must end with a carriage return. If the answer is *yes, check(starter_motor)* succeeds. Otherwise, the goal fails. Characters entered at the keyboard will echo on the screen as they are entered. *Reply* is declared in the domains section as a string or symbol variable. If the answer is *yes, check(starter_motor)* evaluates as *True*.

Another alternative is to use the *readchar* standard predicate. In this case, the example becomes:

```
check(starter_motor):-
  write("Does the starter motor have a ",),nl,
  write("grinding sound (y/n) ?"),nl,
```

```
readchar(Reply),
write(Reply),nl,
Reply='y'.
```

With this predicate, *Reply* must be declared as a character type. There is no echo on the screen, so the *write* predicate with a new line character (*nl*) is necessary to display the answer. It is not necessary to enter any carriage return, and program execution continues after any single character is entered.

If you have many questions in your program, you may want to define your own predicate for the answers:

```
check(starter_motor):-
  write("Does the starter motor have a "),nl,
  write("grinding sound (y/n) ?"),nl,
  response(Reply),
  Reply='y'.
response(Reply):-
  readchar(Reply),
  write(Reply),nl.
```

There are other types of built-in *read* predicates for other domain types:

readchar	Character
readln	String or symbol
readreal	Real number
readint	Integer

For example, we could use the following clauses to read an input value and check the value against a predetermined limit:

```
diagnosed(high_pressure) :-
  check(relief,High),
  High>=250,
  write("Pressure valve is plugged. Clear or"),nl,
  write("replace valve.").

check(X,Pounds) :-
  write("What is the pressure on the ",X,"
  valve?"),
  readint(Pounds).
```

Converting Input

There are also standard predicates for converting input strings to another form. Here are a few Turbo Prolog built-in predicates useful for conversions:

```
upper_lower(Upper,Lower)
```

If *Upper* is bound, *Lower* is bound to the lowercase equivalent. If *Lower* is bound, *Upper* is bound to the uppercase equivalent. If both are bound to the uppercase and lowercase of the same string value, the predicate returns a value of *True*.

```
frontstr(Num,Instring,String1,String2)
```

This example binds *String1* to the first *Num* characters of *Instring;* the remainder of *Instring* is bound to *String2. Instring* must be bound on invocation.

Modifying the Program

We can now modify our simple expert system so that the facts about the problem are entered at execution time. Refer back to the program in listing 6.1. The program asks questions about various symptoms using the *write* predicate, and the answers are retrieved using the *readchar* predicate.

Figure 6.1 shows a sample dialog, with questions and answers. The system now interacts with the user, and the answers are used to set predicates as true or false.

```
Does the engine turn over normally (y/n) ?
n
Are the headlights dim or do they fail to light (y/n) ?
y
Are the battery connections good (y/n) ?
n
Tighten battery connections.
Please press space bar to Exit.
```

Figure 6.1
Sample dialog with the automotive diagnostic expert system

Note: If you experiment with this program, you will find that in most consultations questions are repeated. The program, as yet, has no "memory" to keep track of answers to questions. In the next chapter you will learn how to resolve this problem.

The examples in this chapter are simple examples of what we can do. As we explore more complex examples of data structures in later chapters, you will see how to use variations of these predicates to input data to complex structures, output data from complex structures, and use multichoice questions.

Natural Language Interfaces

Because of its symbolic processing capabilities, Prolog is particularly good for the development of natural language interfaces for expert system programming. For example, the user program might contain:

```
write("What seems to be the problem?"),nl,
readln(Reply).
```

When the program is executing, the user might then answer:

```
The starter motor has a grinding sound.
```

The Prolog program then goes through a *parsing* routine; that is, predicates are used to break the input string into its components. From this, Prolog could eventually define the following clause as true:

```
has(starter_motor,grinding_sound).
```

Exercise

How would you add password control to a Prolog program so that the program prompts for a password and only continues if the password is correct? Write a simple program with password control.

chapter $\boxed{7}$

Using Databases

□ If you experiment with the program in chapter 6, you will soon discover that there are recurring questions when solving most problems. The program does not seem to remember answers to questions. Let's see how we can resolve this problem.

The Problem

Let's suppose, for the moment, that the electrical connections to the battery are at fault. When the program is started, *diagnosed(__)* is first unified with *diagnosed(starter__motor)*. (Refer back to listing 6.1.) The scan of the subgoals starts; the first question asks if the engine is turning over by invoking the predicate *check(engine__turns__over)*. Assuming this is answered *n,* this goal will fail—the motor does not turn over because of the faulty electrical connections. This failure is negated with the *not* predicate, making the test of the condition succeed.

Next, the program tests *check(electrical__power),* asking if the headlights are dim. Assume this is answered *y.* This predicate will fail, causing the goal *diagnosed(starter__motor)* to fail.

The program then unifies *diagnosed(__)* with *diagnosed(battery__ connections),* and the program asks the same questions again to determine if the engine is turning over and whether the headlights are dim. It then asks if the battery connections are good. The program has no way of remembering that it just asked the same questions and that they were answered by the user. What is needed is some type of database in which we can store facts that are discovered true or false.

Databases

The entire Prolog program is really a collection of facts and rules about the relationships of facts. In this sense, the program is really a database. The Prolog language can be viewed as a very powerful query language, selecting facts from the database based on a matching algorithm. The program (as a database) is rather static, however. During a particular consultation you do not add or remove rules that are part of the program. What is needed is some type of dynamic structure to which we can add or remove facts and conclusions during the program's execution.

To resolve our execution problem, Prolog permits the user to add one or more dynamic database structures to the program. You can store what you learn about the problem in these dynamic databases using standard database predicates that are part of Turbo Prolog. In other words, by using database predicates we can add new facts and conclusions to a database during the execution of the program or, conversely, remove facts and conclusions that we previously considered true. The Prolog program has both a *static* and a *dynamic* database.

The Static Database

This database concept is distinctively different from databases used in conventional programming. In conventional programming, information about entities is stored in the database, but any formal rules about relationships of the entities must be "hardwired" into the program.

For example, if you have a program that can configure computers using a conventional database language such as dBASE III, you would store the parts and information about the parts in a database. The rules about how the parts are used, however, are stored as a formal program. Each time the rules are changed or new parts are added, a programmer must rewrite the program.

If you want to make the database "smarter"—capable of storing hierarchical relationships, configuration rules, or relational information—the database quickly becomes unwieldy and program management becomes very difficult and complex.

In contrast, with an expert system designed using Turbo Prolog, the relationships (rules) can be stored in either a static database (the program) or a dynamic database, depending upon the needs of the design.

Let's continue with the example of a program that configures computers. We'll assume that this program configures computer systems for a computer manufacturer. The program must take the customer's specifications and then make up a list of components for a system that meets the specifications. Using a conventional program, the components would be stored in a database. The formal rules about the relationships of the parts are stored as part of the program. For example, a program to configure a network might need a rule that states: if the user plans to install a network, one adapter card is needed for each system. And, for each adapter card, one of four types of cable and its corresponding connector will be needed.

This would work for a while, but what happens as new parts are added and the formal rules change? We can add the parts to the database quickly, but changing the formal rules will take many hours. Updating the program to keep up with the company's products would become a formidable job, even with modern high-level languages such as dBASE III.

With Prolog, updating the program for new components and formal rules is easy. The new rules are added to the database along with the new parts.

The rules and facts that are part of the clauses section of a Turbo Prolog program are a static database. They are compiled as part of the program. They can be edited and the program recompiled, but they are not changed during program execution.

During a Turbo Prolog execution, all of the static database must fit in the computer's memory. This limits the program size to the amount of memory in your system. If your program is too large, consider putting some of the facts in a dynamic database which can, with a little work, be saved as a file and accessed during program execution. Some versions of Prolog (such as Arity's Prolog) permit the use of very large static databases, with part of the program in memory and part on disk. The entire program operates virtually; that is, it functions as though the entire program is in memory. Do not expect good speed from a large program that is partially disk based, however. If that is your only alternative, use a RAMdisk to get as much speed as possible.

The Dynamic Database

If we want to add new facts or conclusions to the program during execution, dynamic databases are defined. This is accomplished by writing database predicates and declaring them as such by using a database section in the program. Normally, you will need at least two database predicates. One of these will be for facts proven true, the other for facts proven false. This chapter will show you how to do this.

With Turbo Prolog, dynamic databases are normally stored entirely in the computer's memory. The computer's memory must be large enough to store all the facts that are needed for a particular consultation. You can save the current dynamic databases to disk (using the standard *save* predicate) or load them from disk to memory (using *consult*). If the dynamic database is too large for the computer's memory, you can use files and your own predicates to permit the use of the large databases.

Declaring Dynamic Databases

Database predicates must be defined in a special database section of the program. This section must precede the predicates section. In our next example, two database predicates—*xpositive(symbol)* and *xnegative (symbol)*—are defined using standard domain types. One of these databases is for facts proven true, the other for facts proven false.

It is also possible to identify field-like entities for the dynamic database. Let's look at a slightly different example using a *person* object for an address database:

```
domains
  name,address,city,state,zip=string
```

```
database
  person(name,address,city,state,zip)
```

This creates a dynamic database predicate—*person*—to which addresses can be added or subtracted during program execution. The predicate is not added to the predicates section because it is already defined in the database section.

Using Dynamic Databases in Expert Systems

After a dynamic database predicate is defined, it can be used in clauses like any other predicate. It is considered true if any match is found in the database, false if no match is found. The expert system program, with the modification for dynamic databases, is shown in listing 7.1. The database predicates are *xpositive* for facts proven true and *xnegative* for facts proven false.

Listing 7.1
Automotive diagnostic system with dynamic database

```
/*      AUTOMOTIVE DIAGNOSTIC SYSTEM
              with dynamic database

        Type RUN in response to the GOAL prompt at runtime.
*/

database
  xpositive(symbol)
  xnegative(symbol)

predicates

  run
```

Listing 7.1 (cont.)

```
diagnosed(symbol)
check(symbol)
positive(string,symbol)
negative(string,symbol)
clear_facts
remember(symbol,char)
ask(string,symbol,char)

clauses

  run:-
    write("AUTOMOBILE DIAGNOSTIC SYSTEM"),nl,
    diagnosed(_),!,nl,clear_facts.

  run:-
    write("\nUnable to determine what"),nl,
    write("your problem is. \n"),clear_facts.

  positive(_,Y) if xpositive(Y),!.
  positive(X,Y) if not(xnegative(Y)) and ask(X,Y,Reply),
   Reply='y'.
  negative(_,Y) if xnegative(Y),!.
  negative(X,Y) if not(xpositive(Y)) and ask(X,Y,Reply),
   Reply='n'.

  ask(X,Y,Reply) :-
    write(X),nl,
    readchar(Reply),
    write(Reply),nl,
    remember(Y,Reply).

  remember(Y,'y'):-
    asserta(xpositive(Y)).

  remember(Y,'n'):-
    asserta(xnegative(Y)).

  clear_facts:-
    retract(xpositive(_)),fail.

  clear_facts:-
    retract(xnegative(_)),fail.

  clear_facts:-
    nl,nl,write("Please press the space bar to
     Exit"),nl,
    readchar(_).
```

Listing 7.1 (cont.)

```
diagnosed(starter_motor) :-
  not(check(engine_turns_over)),
  check(electrical_power),
  check(relay),
  not(check(starter_motor)),
  write("Replace starter motor."),nl.

diagnosed(battery_connections) :-
  not(check(engine_turns_over)),
  not(check(electrical_power)),
  not(check(battery_connections)),
  write("Tighten battery connections."),nl.

diagnosed(battery_water) :-
  not(check(engine_turns_over)),
  not(check(electrical_power)),
  check(battery_connections),
  not(check(battery_water)),
  write("Fill battery with water."),nl.

diagnosed(battery_charged) :-
  not(check(engine_turns_over)),
  not(check(electrical_power)),
  check(battery_connections),
  check(battery_water),
  not(check(battery_charged)),
  write("Battery is not charged. Try jumping it to
    start"),nl,
  write("then check for loose or broken fan
    belt or defective"),nl,
  write("regulator."),nl.

diagnosed(relay) :-
  not(check(engine_turns_over)),
  check(electrical_power),
  not(check(relay)),
  write("Check ignition fuse, key switch, and
    starter motor"),nl,
  write("relay."),nl.

diagnosed(spark_delivery_system) :-
  check(engine_turns_over),
  not(check(spark_delivery_system)),
  write("Check distributor, spark plugs, and
    related wiring."),nl.
```

Listing 7.1 (cont.)

```
diagnosed(fuel_system) :-
  check(engine_turns_over),
  check(spark_delivery_system),
  write("Check gas gauge, fuel filter, and
   possibility of"),nl,
  write("flooding."),nl.

check(battery_connections) :-
  positive("Are the battery connections good (y/n)
   ? ",battery_connections).

check(electrical_power) :-
  negative("Are the headlights dim or do they fail
   to light (y/n) ? ",battery_charged).

check(battery_water) :-
  positive("Is the battery water level good (y/n) ?
   ",battery_water).

check(engine_turns_over) :-
  positive("Does the engine turn over normally
   (y/n) ? ",engine).

check(spark_delivery_system) :-
  positive("Are the spark plug and distributor
   wires good (y/n) ? ",spark).

check(starter_motor) :-
  negative("Does the starter motor fail to
turn,
   turn slowly, or grind (y/n) ? ",motor).

check(relay) :-
  positive("Can you hear the starter motor relay
   pull in (y/n) ? ",relay).

check(battery_charged) :-
  positive("Is the battery fully charged (y/n) ?
   ",battery).
```

Now, in checking each fact, we first invoke the *positive* predicate, which checks the database to see if the answer to the question is already in the database. If the answer is not found, the question is then asked.

After the user answers the question, the answer is stored in the database with the *asserta* predicate, which is a standard predicate. As the user continues the dialog, the dynamic databases grow with new facts learned about the problem. After the problem is solved, the database is cleared with the *retract* predicate, another standard predicate. The program is then ready for the next problem.

Adding or Subtracting from Dynamic Databases

Special standard predicates are used to add new facts to the database or remove facts from the database: *asserta(fact), assertz(fact),* and *retract(fact).* The *asserta(fact)* predicate inserts *fact* at the beginning of a database. The database is viewed as a push-down stack and the new fact is placed on the top of the database. The *assertz(fact)* predicate inserts *fact* at the end of the database. In both cases, variables in *fact* must be bound before the database predicate is invoked. For example, if we want to state that the battery connections are good and this is not the problem, we would use:

```
asserta(xpositive(battery_connections))
```

Note that variables in the database predicate are bound before evaluating *asserta*. The *retract(fact)* standard predicate removes *fact* from the specified database. For example:

```
retract(person("John Jones","Box 45","Acorn","OR",
    "97212"))
```

would remove only John Jones from the database, whereas:

```
retract(person(_,_,_,"OR",_))
```

would remove one *"OR"* item. Any variables not bound when *retract* is invoked will be bound when the predicate is evaluated, making it possible to view each retraction as the fact is removed. For example:

```
retract(person(Person,Address,City,"OR",Zip)
```

would still remove one *"OR"* item, and the variables *Person, Address, City,* and *Zip* would be bound on the removal.

To modify a database (for example, to update an address), the old fact must be removed and the new fact inserted. You do not edit an existing fact in the database.

With an expert system, a dynamic database is used to store facts about a particular problem. After the problem is solved, the database must be cleared (using *retract*) to store the facts about the next problem. In this example, the *clear_facts* predicate is used to clear the database with *retract*.

Saving Dynamic Databases

With Turbo Prolog, you can save facts in a dynamic database to a file and use this file with the program or other programs at a later time. To save a dynamic database as a disk file, use the *save* predicate with the name you want to give the file, such as:

```
save("auto.dat")
```

The resulting file will be a collection of facts, much like the clauses section of any program.

To read these facts into the program or another program later, use the *consult* predicate:

```
consult("auto.dat").
```

This predicate returns the value of *True,* after which all of the facts in *auto.dat* will become part of the current program.

Remember again that dynamic databases saved or read must fit into memory with the program and other clauses (static database). The number of rules and facts in both databases is limited by the amount of your computer's memory.

Using Large Databases

Sometimes you may want to create a very large dynamic database that can't fit in memory. In this case, you create the dynamic database as a random-access file (with an index) on a disk. You then create predicates that use the disk file to verify a fact, just as you use standard predicates to verify a fact in memory. The Turbo Prolog manual includes details on how to do this and listings for these disk access predicates.

Exercises

1. In the examples using the *person* predicate in this chapter, the fields were defined as string type rather than symbol. Why did we do this? Try an example both ways and see what happens.

2. Modify the automobile diagnostic routine for the dynamic databases as described in this chapter. Execute a few sample diagnostics and describe how the databases help execution.

3. Add a *save("test.dat")* predicate just before the *clear_facts* predicate in the first *run* clause in the automobile diagnostic routine. Execute an example, then exit Turbo Prolog and examine the TEST.DAT file. What does it contain?

chapter $\boxed{8}$

Controlling the
Flow of Execution

☐ Prolog pursues a relentless search to solve a goal, winding like the video game centipede through the rules until it can prove or disprove a goal. If one path fails, Prolog backtracks and tries another. The proof of the goal becomes an elusive quarry, with Prolog always in pursuit until the goal is satisfied or all matching clauses have been tested.

In many applications, however, you want to control backtracking. You may either want to terminate or force backtracking based on a certain goal being true or false. This chapter will look at ways you can control backtracking.

The Cut

The cut is a predicate that can be used to prevent backtracking based on a specified condition. It is written as an exclamation point (*!*) and can be used for any or all of the following three purposes:

1. To terminate the search for further solutions of a goal after the goal has been satisfied. For example, after we have satisfied *diagnosed(X)* in our diagnostic program, we can terminate our search for more solutions. There is only one answer, and after it has been found the search can be stopped.

2. To terminate the search for a solution of a goal after the goal

has failed. The cut is used with the *fail* standard predicate to force the failure of the goal and terminate the search for further solutions (see next section).

3. To indicate to the program that the correct clause for a predicate has been chosen and there is no need to check further clauses. In effect, you are saying: "If you get here, you have found the correct rule and there is no need to check further rules with the same predicate."

A Cut Example

Let's look, for the moment, at the diagnostic program:

```
run :-
  write("AUTOMOBILE DIAGNOSTIC PROGRAM"),nl,
  diagnosed(_),!,clear_facts.

run:-
  write("Unable to determine your problem."),nl,
  clear_facts.
```

In this example, the cut is indicated by the exclamation point in the first clause after *diagnosed(_)*. As a predicate, the cut always succeeds. The program is initiated by specifying *run* as a goal. This matches the first clause, so Prolog writes the title and then tries to prove the next subgoal, *diagnosed(_)*. The first match for this in the program will be *diagnosed(starter_motor)*. If this fails, the program continues, trying to prove *diagnosed(battery_connections)*. This continues until the subgoal *diagnosed(_)* is satisfied.

After this subgoal is satisfied, the *run* clause reaches the cut. This effectively acts as a fence. After this fence is crossed the program cannot backtrack over the fence. All pointers and markers before the fence are lost, releasing memory space for more markers and pointers.

After *diagnosed(_)* is proven true, the program cannot backtrack and ask additional questions to solve another *diagnosed(_)* predicate, nor can it backtrack to try the second *run* clause.

From a programming perspective, the cut saves both memory space and execution time because markers are released and backtracking is terminated. From the user's perspective, execution is faster. In addition, because nonrelevant goals are not pursued, only questions that are specifically related to the problem are asked. Without the cut, the program would always ask all the questions in all the rules in trying to satisfy additional goals.

Using the Cut

The cut—one of the most complex features of Prolog—is essential to efficiently control the execution of most programs. Several examples should help clarify its use.

As a general case, suppose we have the rule:

```
q :- x and y and z and ! and a and b and c.
```

Prolog will try to prove *q* by backtracking between *x, y,* and *z* as many times as necessary until *x, y,* and *z* are all true. After this takes place, the cut is reached (which always evaluates as true).

After the cut is crossed, Prolog cannot go back across the cut. The program will try to prove *a,* then *b,* then *c.* If *a* fails, the program cannot backtrack and prove *x, y,* or *z* with new bindings. If *a* fails, *q* fails. The program can backtrack between *a, b,* and *c* but not to *z.* If *a, b,* or *c* fails, *q* will fail. The markers for *x, y,* and *z* are lost after the cut is crossed. All variables in *x, y,* and *z* are bound when the cut is reached and Prolog is committed to all choices before the cut after *q* was invoked.

Another Cut Example

In our diagnostic program routine, there is another example of a cut:

```
positive(_,Y) if xpositive(Y),!.
positive(X,Y) if
  not(xnegative(Y)),ask(X,Y),Reply='y'.
```

In this routine, the program first checks to see if the fact is in the database. If found, the cut is invoked. Because the cut always succeeds, the clause succeeds. The cut prevents backtracking and checking the second *positive(X,Y)* clause, even if the rule that invoked *positive(__, Y)* fails. After the cut is reached, the program is committed to the first clause.

Not let's expand this feature further. In our current example, you are limited to a single line of text in the question and no additional variables. Suppose we wish to use multiple variables and several lines of text? The following example uses the cut to support this modification:

```
check(fan,110,Z) :-
  motor_voltage(fan,110,Z),
  Z='y'.

motor_voltage(X,Volts,Z) :-
  xmotor_voltage(X,Volts,'y'),!,Z='y'.

motor_voltage(X,Volts,Z) :-
  xmotor_voltage(X,Volts,'n'),!,Z='n'.

motor_voltage(X,Volts,Z) :-
  write("Is there ",Volts," volts at "),nl,
  write( X," motor (y/n) ? "),
```

```
      answer(Reply),
      asserta(xmotor_voltage(fan,Volts,Reply)),
      Z=Reply.

answer(Reply) :-
  readchar(Reply),
  write(Reply),nl.
```

In this example:

```
xmotor_voltage(symbol,integer,char)
```

is the single database predicate used. The predicate *motor_voltage* is the conclusion of three clauses. When the goal *check(fan,110,_)* is invoked, the first *motor_voltage* predicate checks to see if:

```
xmotor_voltage(fan,110,'y')
```

is in the database. If found, the rule succeeds and the cut prevents checking the second and third rule with the same head. If this fails, a check is made to see if:

```
xmotor_voltage(fan,110,'n')
```

is in the database. If found, this clause succeeds and the cut prevents the check of the next clause if backtracking is necessary. If neither answer is found in the database, the user is asked the question. The answer is placed in the database.

The Fail Predicate

There are times when you may want a goal to fail if the program gets to that point. In effect, you want to force backtracking. We use the standard *fail* predicate to force backtracking. The predicate has no arguments, which means that the success or failure of the rule of which it is a part does not depend on the value to which a variable is bound. The rule always fails if it reaches that point. In Prolog, failure is not a negative concept. It is a form of control, and is very important for the design of efficient programs.

A Fail Example

For example, we could force a failure of a response predicate if the answer is negative:

```
ask(X,Y) :-
  write(Y),nl,
```

```
    readchar(Reply),
    write(Reply),nl,
    remember(X,Reply).

remember(X,'y') :-
  asserta(xpositive(X)).

remember(X,'n') :-
  asserta(xnegative(X)),fail.
```

If the answer is negative, *remember* fails, forcing the failure of *ask,* which in turn forces the failure of the predicate calling *ask* if there are no additional predicates of the same name through which Prolog can backtrack.

In some cases, you may want to use the *fail* predicate with a cut to force backtracking. The cut forces binding of a variable at a particular point in proving a rule. After this is accomplished, you can check other subgoals, finally using the *fail* predicate to force failure for that particular binding.

For example, assume that we have a database of addresses and we want to eliminate some names from the database. You select an address, then proceed to test various goals on that address. The *fail* predicate is used to exclude addresses not desired. We could eliminate addresses that are in Oregon with:

```
person(_,_,_,state,_):- person(_,_,_,"OR",_),fail.
```

Using a Fail to Get Multiple Goal States

In some cases, you may have a program in which the goal succeeds with multiple facts or rules. For example, suppose the goal is specified as *diagnosed(X)* for the automotive diagnostic system and both the starter motor and battery have been diagnosed as defective by previous rules. You want both answers displayed.

If you are compiling and executing the program internal to Turbo Prolog, all solutions are displayed automatically. But if you compile the program for external execution, only the first answer is displayed. You can, however, use the *fail* predicate to force the display of all answers in a compiled program:

```
run :-
  diagnosed(X),
  write("The ",X," is defective"),nl,
  fail.

run.
```

```
diagnosed(starter_motor).

diagnosed(battery).
```

For the sake of simplicity, the *diagnosed* predicates are shown as simple facts. When *run* is invoked as a goal, the program tries to solve *diagnosed(X),* binding *X* first to *starter_motor.* This will succeed and the first diagnosis will be displayed. The *run* clause then fails because of the *fail* predicate, which forces backtracking and another attempt to solve *diagnosed(X).* It will succeed again and the second diagnosis will be displayed. Again, the *fail* predicate forces backtracking. There are no more solutions, so the *run* clause fails. This forces backtracking to the second *run* clause, which always succeeds.

Using the Cut and Fail

The *!* (cut) and *fail* predicates are often used together to control program execution. As a summary, the cut and *fail* predicates can serve any of three purposes in a program:

1. The cut optimizes code. Using the cut, you may be able to use fewer clauses. If, for example, a condition is common to several rules, put that condition in a separate rule with cut and *fail* predicates. Suppose you want to eliminate applicants under the age of 21:

```
eligible(X) :-
  age(X,Y),Y<21,!,fail.

eligible(X) :- major(X,computer_science).

eligible(X) :- major(X,electrical_engineering).

interview(X) :-
  ...
  eligible(X)
  write(X)...,fail.
```

If the applicant is 21 or over, the *eligible(X)* predicate will fail at *Y<21* and the program immediately backtracks and tests the next clause. The goal succeeds if either of the next two clauses is true (applicant majored in electrical engineering or computer science). If the applicant is under 21, the cut is invoked. The *fail* predicate forces the failure of the rule and the cut prevents backtracking. You could have many OR conditions here, each added with a separate rule. The one common requirement (age) is a part of each premise (ANDed).

2. The cut enables you to control program execution. In the previous example, if the applicant had both degrees, the name would be

displayed twice. You can prevent this duplication by adding a second cut:

```
eligible(X) :-
  age(X,Y),Y<21,!,fail.

eligible(X) :- major(X,computer_science),!.

eligible(X) :- major(X,electrical_engineering).

interview(X) :-
  ...
  eligible(X)
  write(X)...,fail.
```

3. Cuts improve the efficiency of program execution. By using the cut to eliminate clauses that do not need to be checked, execution is faster.

A Word of Caution

Both the cut and the fail are a type of control, forcing the program to a particular type of execution. Cuts force binding, clear markers, and commit the program to particular clauses. Used correctly, the cut and the fail are a valuable type of control. Control in any form, however, is a type of knowledge. In using the cut and fail, you are forcing structure and a form of knowledge into the expert system. You must always be sure that this structure (which is a type of procedural control) matches the reality of the domain represented by the expert system. Cuts and fails used improperly can cause strange program execution.

Exercises

1. Enter and test the following program. What is the output if *run* is specified as a goal? Explain the logic flow.

```
run :-
  test.
run :-
  write("End of test 1").

test :-
  get_data,
  write("End of test 2").
test :-
  nl,write("END"),nl.
```

```
get_data :-
  go,
  data(X),
  write(X),fail.
get_data :-
  nl,write("END OF DATA"),nl.

go :-
  write("BEGIN"),nl.
go :-
  write("TRY AGAIN"),nl.

data("This").
data("is").
data("a").
data("test").
```

2. Place a cut after the *data(X)* predicate in *get_data*. What is the output now? Explain the new logic flow.

```
get_data :-
  go,
  data(X),!,
  write(X),fail.
```

3. Try the cut at other places, noting where each cut is placed and the resulting output.

chapter $\boxed{9}$

Using Complex Data Structures: Compound Structures and Lists

☐ Turbo Prolog permits you to create complex data structures and nonstandard domain types. In this chapter, you will learn how to use these in building expert systems.

Compound Structures

With Turbo Prolog, you can create objects that can contain other objects. This permits the definition of hierarchical relationships between objects.

Let's suppose an automobile has several fans and we want to include a single diagnostic routine in our expert system for all of these fans. We could simplify our programming by defining an automobile fan as a compound structure in our diagnostic system as:

```
fan(radiator)
```

and then create a clause with the head:

```
check(fan(Y),turning):-
  write("Is the ",Y," fan turning (y/n) ?"),...
```

We could then use rules with this conclusion to check several types of fans by binding *Y* to different values: radiator, heater, or whatever fan we are checking.

In this example, *fan(Y)* is a *compound structure*. The first part of the compound structure is the *functor.* The part of the structure within the parentheses is the *component.* In this case, *fan* is the functor and *radiator* is the component. We can use the same clause to check several types of fans by binding the component to different values:

```
check(fan(Y),turning):-
```

The hierarchical relationship can be expressed as shown in figure 9.1. The predicate functions on the compound structure as though it were a single object.

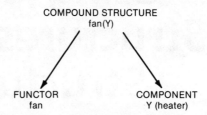

Figure 9.1
The compound structure

You can use multiple components with a compound structure if you wish:

```
likes(book("Mastering Expert Systems with Turbo Prolog",
    "Carl Townsend","SAMS","1987")).
```

The Advantages of Using Compound Structures

Using compound structures offer several advantages in Prolog programming:

1. Compound structures permit you to simplify programming by reducing the number of rules necessary. For example, suppose you are writing an expert system for a system with five motors. You could write a single set of rules for diagnosing problems relevant to all five motors, using a compound structure to distinguish between the types of motors being diagnosed. The one set of rules could then test all the motors. For example:

```
check(fan(Y),turning):-
   write("Is the ",Y," turning (y/n) ? "),
   ask(Reply),Reply='y'.
```

2. Compound structures permit you to treat related information

as a single object. An address, for example, may contain a name, street, city, state, and zip code. Defined as a compound structure, the address could be treated as a single object while maintaining the relationship between the parts of the address. This is somewhat like database management, except that the structures can be hierarchical.

3. Compound structures are useful when there are many types of one object. For example, we could state:

```
owns(bill,book).
owns(jack,book).
```

This expresses the fact that Jack and Bill each own a book, but does not tell us if they own the same book or different books. We could clarify this by specifying the title of the book as:

```
owns(bill,"Gone with the Wind").
owns(jack,"Dune").
```

This has a problem in that it does not tell us whether the title is owned as a book or as a videotape. We could, however, express the fact that the titles are owned as books using:

```
owns(bill,book("Gone with the Wind")).
owns(jack,book("Dune")).
```

Declaring Compound Structures

When you use a compound structure, you are creating a new data type and each part of the structure must be defined in the domains section. The domains and predicates for the last example of the last section would be:

```
domains
  article=book(title); video(title); computer
  title=string
  person=symbol

predicates
  owns(person,article)
```

This defines a new domain type *article*. The semicolon is read as an *OR* operator, and the expression is read "article can be a book, video, or computer." Each declaration within the parentheses must be of a standard domain type (for example, symbol or string) or defined elsewhere in the domains section, as we did in this example.

We could then express as clauses:

```
owns(bill,book("Gone with the Wind")).
owns(jack,book("Dune")).
owns(mary,video("Ghostbusters")).
owns(bill,computer).
```

If you now invoked the goal:

```
owns(bill,X)
```

you would receive the answers:

```
X=book("Gone with the Wind")
X=computer
```

Notice in this case *computer* is a compound structure (and functor) without a component.

Using Multiple Levels

Components of compound structures are similar to database fields, but they are a much more powerful concept. Unlike database fields, compound structures can be extended in hierarchical relationships, making the components functors in other compound structures. For example:

```
teaching(class(student(name,address),class_number),
    professor)
```

This would permit us to query if a teaching relationship exists between a professor, class, and student in the class. Refer to figure 9.2. You can, therefore, express a hierarchical relationship between objects using compound structures.

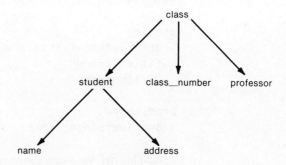

Figure 9.2
A compound structure example

Following are some examples of compound structures:

```
address(name,street,city,state,zip)
```

```
car(1970,1971,1972)
products(software,hardware)
clients(teachers,principals,school_related)
products(software(spreadsheet,word_processing),books)
```

Each argument of the compound structure expresses a subdivision or part of the whole.

With Turbo Prolog, you cannot compare compound structures for equality using the = operator. To compare compound structures, create an *equal* predicate as follows:

```
equal(X,X).
```

List Structures

Lists are another common type of data structure in symbolic programming. A *list* is an ordered sequence of terms that can have any length. The word *ordered* is important because it indicates that the order of the terms is important.

The List

Lists are expressed using brackets, with the components of the list separated by commas:

```
scores([2,7,2,9,4]).
```

This is a fact that defines a list called *scores* that consists of the numbers *2,7,2,9,4* in the specified order. The components of a list can be symbols, strings, characters, numbers, compound structures, or another list. All components, however, should be of the same domain type. You can also define a null or empty list by using only the two brackets:

```
costs([]).
```

The list structure has two components, a *head* and a *tail*. The head is the first term or element of the list. The tail is the list that remains if the head is removed. If there are no more elements to be removed, the tail is an empty list.

For example, in the list:

```
names([jack,bill,sue,mary,george]).
```

jack is the head of the list and *[bill,sue,mary,george]* is the tail. (Notice that the head is a simple object and the tail is a list.) The items of the list are placed between brackets to indicate that they are in a list. The same fact can be expressed as:

```
names(jack¦[bill,sue,mary,george]).
```

Notice the vertical bar (¦), which indicates that the list is expressed as a head and a tail. If we use the goal *names([X¦ Y]*, the variable *X* would be bound to *jack* and *Y* would be bound to *[bill,sue,mary,george]*. The tail of a list with a single element is an empty list.

Declaring Lists

As with compound structures, lists are a special type of data structure and must be declared in the domains section. All terms in a list must be of the same type, but can be lists or compound structures if desired.

Suppose, as an example, we want to define the various diagnostic possibilities for our automotive expert system as a list. These are each a hypothesis and the program will be modified to check each in turn. In other words, we have the list:

```
possibilities([
   starter_motor,
   battery_connections,
   battery_water,
   battery_charged,
   ignition,
   spark_delivery_system,
   fuel_system,
]).
```

We will call this list the hypotheses list. We now add the domains and predicates sections:

```
domains
   hlist=hypothesis*
   hypothesis=symbol

predicates
   possibilities(hlist)
```

Notice that the type designator ends in an asterisk to indicate it is a list. The same word appears in the domains section without the asterisk to define the domain type for the members of the list (*symbol* in this example).

Using Lists

Our program can then be modified to permit using this list to control the flow of the program:

```
run:-
```

```
    write("AUTOMOBILE DIAGNOSTIC SYSTEM"),nl,
    possibilities(X),
    run1(X).

run1([]) :-
    write("Unable to determine what"),nl,
    write("your problem is."),nl,clear_facts.

run1([Head|Tail]) :-
    Y=Head,diagnosed(Y),!,nl,clear_facts.

run1([Head|Tail]) :-
    !,run1(Tail).
```

Now let's look at how this modification works. When the program is started, the variable *X* is bound to the list and *run1* is invoked. The first *run1* clause fails because the list is not empty. The second *run1* clause is then invoked.

A list, as mentioned, can also be represented by a head and a tail, or:

```
[Head|Tail]
```

where *Head* and *Tail* could be any variables that represent the head and tail of the list, respectively. *Head* is initially bound to *starter_motor,* the first item on the list. The goal *diagnosed(starter_motor)* is then invoked. If this succeeds, the cut is invoked to prevent backtracking and execution of the third *run1.* If *diagnosed(starter_motor)* fails, the goal *run1* fails and the third *run1* clause is invoked. This automatically succeeds, invoking the cut. The last *run1* predicate then invokes *run1,* which invokes the first *run1* predicate again with the previous tail as the argument.

> **Note:** It is important to see that the third *run1* clause does not backtrack. It calls *run1* in a process called *recursion,* which will be explained in more depth in the next chapter. For now, it is only necessary to see that a predicate in Turbo Prolog can invoke a copy of itself.

If you want to try this modification in the program, you must be sure to add a clause defining the list and the *run1* predicate to the predicates list. The entire program using the list data structure is shown in listing 9.1.

Listing 9.1
Automotive diagnostic system with dynamic database and list

```
/*      AUTOMOTIVE DIAGNOSTIC SYSTEM
            with dynamic database and list
```

Listing 9.1 (cont.)
Type RUN in response to the GOAL prompt at runtime.
*/

```
domains
  hlist=hypothesis*
  hypothesis=symbol

database
  xpositive(symbol)
  xnegative(symbol)

predicates
  run
  run1(hlist)
  possibilities(hlist)
  diagnosed(symbol)
  check(symbol)
  positive(string,symbol)
  negative(string,symbol)
  clear_facts
  remember(symbol,char)
  ask(string,symbol,char)

clauses

  run :-
    write("AUTOMOBILE DIAGNOSTIC SYSTEM"),nl,
    possibilities(X),run1(X).

  run1([]) :-
    write("\nUnable to determine what"),nl,
    write("your problem is. \n"),clear_facts.

  run1([H|_]) :-
    Y=H,diagnosed(Y),!,nl,clear_facts.

  run1([_|Tail]) :-
    !,run1(Tail).

  positive(_,Y) if xpositive(Y),!.
  positive(X,Y) if not(xnegative(Y)) and ask(X,Y,Reply),
    Reply='y'.
  negative(_,Y) if xnegative(Y),!.
  negative(X,Y) if not(xpositive(Y)) and ask(X,Y,Reply),
    Reply='n'.

  ask(X,Y,Reply) :-
```

Listing 9.1 (cont.)

```prolog
  write(X),nl,
  readchar(Reply),
  write(Reply),nl,
  remember(Y,Reply).

remember(Y,'y'):-
  asserta(xpositive(Y)).

remember(Y,'n'):-
  asserta(xnegative(Y)).

clear_facts:-
  retract(xpositive(_)),fail.

clear_facts:-
  retract(xnegative(_)),fail.

clear_facts:-
  nl,nl,write("Please press the space bar to
   Exit"),nl,
  readchar(_).

possibilities([
  starter_motor,
  battery_connections,
  battery_water,
  battery_charged,
  relay,
  spark_delivery_system,
  fuel_system
]).

diagnosed(starter_motor) :-
  not(check(engine_turns_over)),
  check(electrical_power),
  check(relay),
  not(check(starter_motor)),
  write("Replace starter motor."),nl.

diagnosed(battery_connections) :-
  not(check(engine_turns_over)),
  not(check(electrical_power)),
  not(check(battery_connections)),
  write("Tighten battery connections."),nl.

diagnosed(battery_water) :-
  not(check(engine_turns_over)),
```

Listing 9.1 (cont.)

```
    not(check(electrical_power)),
    check(battery_connections),
    not(check(battery_water)),
    write("Fill battery with water."),nl.

diagnosed(battery_charged) :-
    not(check(engine_turns_over)),
    not(check(electrical_power)),
    check(battery_connections),
    check(battery_water),
    not(check(battery_charged)),
    write("Battery is not charged. Try jumping it to
      start"),nl,
    write("then check for loose or broken fan belt or
      defective"),nl,
    write("regulator."),nl.

diagnosed(relay) :-
    not(check(engine_turns_over)),
    check(electrical_power),
    not(check(relay)),
    write("Check ignition fuse, key switch, and starter
      motor"),nl,
    write("relay."),nl.

diagnosed(spark_delivery_system) :-
    check(engine_turns_over),
    not(check(spark_delivery_system)),
    write("Check distributor, spark plugs, and related
      wiring."),nl.

diagnosed(fuel_system) :-
    check(engine_turns_over),
    check(spark_delivery_system),
    write("Check gas gauge, fuel filter, and possibility
      of"),nl,
    write("flooding."),nl.

check(battery_connections) :-
    positive("Are the battery connections good (y/n) ?
      ",battery_connections).

check(electrical_power) :-
    negative("Are the headlights dim or do they fail to
      light (y/n) ? ",battery_charged).

check(battery_water) :-
```

Listing 9.1 (cont.)

```
positive("Is the battery water level good (y/n) ?
    ",battery_water).

check(engine_turns_over) :-
  positive("Does the engine turn over normally (y/n) ?
    ",engine).

check(spark_delivery_system) :-
  positive("Are the spark plug and distributor wires
    good (y/n) ? ",spark).

check(starter_motor) :-
  negative("Does the starter motor fail to turn, turn
    slowly, or grind (y/n) ? ",motor).

check(relay) :-
  positive("Can you hear the starter motor relay pull
    in (y/n) ? ",relay).

check(battery_charged) :-
  positive("Is the battery fully charged (y/n) ?
    ",battery).
```

Without the list, the order in which the diagnosis proceeds is controlled by the order of the *diagnosed(X)* clauses in the program. To change the diagnosis order, you must reorder these clauses. With the list, you can now control the order in which the diagnosis proceeds by reordering the list. It is also easier to see the list of possible diagnostic causes.

Lists are often very important data structures in Prolog programming. General-purpose predicates can be set up with variables, testing for a condition within the predicate. The resulting predicates are "driven" from a list to find which values of the list succeed with the predicate. Lists can be used as constraints in expert system design. Instead of checking to see if a value is between certain limits, you can check to see if the value is in a list (such as a list of colors).

The next chapter will introduce the topic of recursion in more depth and the relationship of lists to recursion. Recursion techniques are extremely useful with lists, because these techniques are used to determine if an object is part of a list, to append one list to another, and to print a list.

Lists are not the same as vectors or matrices. A vector (one-dimensional matrix) or matrix is a static and homogeneous structure that permits relatively fast access to any member of the structure. Lists are dynamic and nonhomogeneous, but access is less efficient (see table 9.1).

Table 9.1
Matrices and Lists

Matrices	Lists
Fixed length and depth	Variable length and depth
Easy to access specific location	Difficult to access specific location
Static structure during execution	Dynamic structure during execution
Homogeneous data types must be used	Lists, variables, constants, and compound structures can be mixed in lists

Exercises

1. Lists are one of the most important data structures in Prolog programming. Why is this true?

2. Identify the head and the tail of each list:

    a. scores([85,96,75,87,94,98,91])

    b. colors([blue,red,black,green,white])

    c. names([bob,sue,mary,bill,tom,elaine,george])

3. Write each of the lists in example 2 using XXX([Head ¦ Tail]) notation.

4. Enter and execute the program in listing 9.1.

5. Write a short program using the following as a compound structure:

```
address(name,street,city,state,zip)
```

Write an input routine that can be used to enter values to each part of the compound structure, creating a dynamic database. (Hint: Each part must be entered with a separate input predicate.)

chapter 10

Special Prolog Techniques

☐ This chapter introduces several Prolog techniques that are important in building successful expert systems. These techniques include recursion, advanced input and output, the *repeat* predicate, and arithmetical operations.

Recursion

In the last chapter, you were introduced to an example of *recursion*. Recursion is a technique in which an entity is defined in terms of itself. In a Prolog program, recursion is the technique of using a clause to invoke a copy of itself. Recursion is essential for most expert system programming and almost any type of list processing.

Look again at the example of recursion in the third *run1* clause of listing 9.1. In this example, *run1* appears to invoke itself. More accurately, however, we could say that *run1* invokes a copy of itself. There is no backward movement or retracing. In fact, the cut before the recursion prevents that.

Counting

One of the most common uses of recursion is to implement a counter. If you need a counter in a Prolog program, the traditional programming method will not work. For example, the following Prolog program will *not* work:

```
test :-
  X = 5,
  X = X + 1,
  write(X),nl.
```

If you try this, the rule starts by binding X to 5. The rule then fails at $X = X + 1$; this is simply a test because X is already bound. The last part of the rule is never reached.

The proper solution is to use recursion and backtracking to implement the counter:

```
test(10).
test(X) :-
  Y = X + 1,
  write(Y),nl,test(Y).
```

When the goal *test(5)* is specified, the program starts by finding a match on the second rule, binding X to 5. The variable Y is then bound to $X + 1$ and displayed. Again, there is then a recursive call to the *test* predicate. The program continues until the variable value reaches 10, after which the execution is terminated by the first rule. A variable is only bound for the current clause, but in a recursive call the clause invoked is a new clause. The Y in *test(Y)* is bound to 6 in the first cycle, forcing a binding of X to 6 in the recursive call.

Terminating Recursive Loops

When using a recursive definition, you must always define a terminating condition or the program will recurse forever. Normally, this terminating control is the first predicate of a group of common clauses containing the recursive definition.

Try again, with a slight modification, the example in the last section:

```
test(9).
test(X) :-
  Y = X + 1,
  write(Y),test(Y),
  write(" END ").
```

If you try this with the goal *test(5),* you will see the following output:

```
6789 END   END   END   END
```

on the screen. The program winds downward through the recursive calls, outputting each number. The final *write* is never reached in this downward recursion. After the terminating condition is met, however, each call must unwind, moving upward through the recursive calls and invoking the final statement on each call.

To see this more dramatically, change the program to:

```
test(9).
test(X) :-
  Y = X + 1,
  test(Y),write(Y),
  write(" END ").
```

Now the entire operation of the program is changed. The output now becomes:

9 END 8 END 7 END 6 END

The numbers are in descending order because the output is from the unwinding or backing out of the recursive calls. From this we can state the following rule for recursion in designing Prolog programs.

> **Recursion Rule:** If the recursive call is not the last condition of the rule, Prolog invokes each of the remaining conditions as it unwinds from the recursion.

A Word of Caution

Recursion is essential in most programs, but it should be used with caution. Some general guidelines follow.

1. Recursive calls require memory if the recursive call is not the last premise in the rule. The program has to mark the return location and save all variables that are part of the current clause, because these variables will be active on the return. If you only need a way to repeat, backtrack with the *fail* predicate instead of using recursion.

2. Recursion adds complexity to the program. It is not a simple concept. The flow of execution is difficult to visualize and errors are more difficult to find.

3. If possible, make the recursive procedure do its work on the way down instead of the way up.

4. Minimize variables and complex structures in the recursion.

Checking for List Membership

Another use of recursion is to see if an item is a member of a list. For example, suppose we have a list of names and we want to see if a name is a member of the list. To do this, we could create the following short program:

```
domains
  namelist=name*
  name=string

predicates
  member(name,namelist)

clauses
  member(Name,[Name|_]).
  member(Name,[_|Tail]) if
  member(Name,Tail).
```

You could then specify as a goal:

```
member("John Doe",["Mary Smith","John Doe","Robert
    Hill"])
```

The first clause succeeds if *John Doe* is the head of the list. Otherwise, the first clause will fail and Prolog then tries the next clause. The second clause checks to see if *John Doe* is a member of the tail. This clause uses recursion to check if *John Doe* is at the beginning of the tail. If this fails, the recursion checks to see if *John Doe* is in the remaining tail. The process continues until the list is empty, unless the name is found and the goal succeeds.

Outputting Lists

If you have a list that you want to display or print, you cannot use normal output commands with the list because the list is not a standard domain type. You can, however, create your own output predicate for a list using the standard *write* predicate and recursion:

```
write_list([]).
write_list([Head|Tail]) :-
  write(Head),nl,write_list(Tail).
```

Combining Lists

If you want to add one list to another list, you can create your own *append* predicate:

```
append(List1,List2,List3)
```

where *List3* is the result of combining *List2* to the end of *List1*. The predicate can be defined as:

```
append([],List2,List2).
append([X|L1],List2,[X|L3]) :-
  append(L1,List2,L3).
```

This predicate has a variety of applications. It can be used to find an output list given two input lists. Conversely, if we know the output list and one of the input lists, they can be used to find the other input list. Refer to table 10.1 for examples of useful predicates for list operations.

Table 10.1
List Operations

Outputting Lists

```
write_list([]).
write_list([Head|Tail]) :-
  write(Head),nl,write_list(Tail).
```

Combining Lists

```
append([],List2,List2).
append([X|L1],List2,[X|L3]) :-
  append(L1,List2,L3).
```

Find nth Member of List

```
nth(X,1,[X|_]).
nth(X,N,[_|L]) :-
  R=N-1,
    nth(X,R,L).
```

Find Last Element of List

```
last(X,[X]).
last(X,[_|L]) :- last(X,L).
```

Bubble Sort

```
bubblesort(L,S) :-
    append(X,[A,B|Y],L),
    order(B,A),
    append(X,[B,A|Y],M),
    bubblesort(M,S),!.
bubblesort(L,L).
order(A,B) :- A<B.
```

The Repeat Predicate

The *repeat* predicate can be used to force a program to generate alternative solutions through backtracking. Each time backtracking returns you to the *repeat* predicate, *repeat* succeeds and subsequent goals may provide different variable values.

The *repeat* predicate is not a standard predicate in Turbo Prolog and it must be added to your program. It has the following form:

```
repeat.
repeat :- repeat.
```

Let's see how the *repeat* predicate works. The startup routines in our program can be modified to:

```
run :-
  repeat,
  run_once,
  clear_facts,
  write("Would you like another consultation? "),
  readchar(Reply),
  write(Reply),nl,
  Reply='n'.

run_once :-
  title,
  diagnosed(Y),
  nl,!,
  clear_facts.

run_once :-
  write("\nUnable to determine what"),nl
  write("your problem is. \n"),clear_facts.
```

When *run* is invoked, *repeat* will succeed the first time through because of the first *repeat* clause, which is always true. If *run_once* succeeds, the value of *Y* is bound and the diagnosis is displayed. The question is asked for another consultation. If the answer is *y,* the *run* predicate fails and the program backtracks to *repeat.*

After the program backtracks to the *repeat* predicate, the second *repeat* clause is tried, which is a rule. The rule is recursive, invoking the first *repeat* clause again, which will succeed. Prolog then moves forward again on the new path—invoking *run_once* again—and the loop continues. In fact, the loop can continue until the user answers the question with *n,* forcing the *run* predicate to succeed and backtracking to terminate.

The repeat loop follows this general method of operation:

1. After the *repeat* predicate is invoked, Prolog continues to solve subgoals until a subgoal fails.

2. After a subgoal fails, Prolog backtracks to the *repeat* predicate and tries to prove the subgoals again.

There must be some method within the loop to ensure that the variable that controls the termination test can be changed. Otherwise, you will have an infinite loop (one that continues forever). In this example, the *readchar* predicate controls the input variable *Reply,* which controls termination.

Using Multichoice Questions

The *repeat* predicate can also be used to create a multichoice questions predicate and eliminate illegal values. For example:

```
check(Z,X) :-
  dbase(Z,Y),X=Y,!.

check(starter_motor,X) :-
  not(dbase(system,_),
  repeat,
  write("Which of the following is true of the"),nl,
  write("starter motor? "),nl,
  write(" 1)   The starter motor does not turn "),nl,
  write("      at all."),nl,
  write(" 2)   The starter motor turns over "),nl,
  write("      slowly."),nl,
  write(" 3)   The starter motor turns over "),nl,
  write("      with a grinding sound."),nl,
  write(" 4)   The starter motor turns over "),nl,
  write("      normally,"),nl,
  write("SELECT: "),nl,
  readchar(Reply),write(Reply),nl,
  char_int(Reply,Z),
  Z>48,Z<53,
  asserta(starter_motor,Reply),
  X=Reply.
```

The *check* predicate is called with the desired option:

```
diagnosed(starter_motor) :-
  (check(starter_motor,'1'),
  write("Power is not getting to the"),nl,
  write("starter motor.").
```

The first *check* predicate checks to see if *starter_motor,'1'* is in the database from a previous query. If so, the goal succeeds and *diagnosed(starter_motor)* displays the diagnostic message.

If there is no database entry or the database entry unifies with the first argument but fails on the second argument, the first *check* predicate fails and Prolog backtracks to the second *check* predicate.

The second *check* predicate first checks the database to see if anything in the database unifies with the first argument. If so, it indicates that the menu has been displayed before and the user selected an option at that time. In this case, the *check* predicate fails and the cut on the first *check* predicate prevents any backtracking. If the database has no entry for this argument, the menu is displayed for an option selection.

101

Any of four options can be selected. At the beginning of the menu predicate, a check is first made to see if any option has already been stored in the database. The standard predicate *char_int* binds *Z* to the ASCII value of the option entered (49 through 52). If this value is greater than 52 or less than 48, the goal fails and the program backtracks to *repeat,* displaying the options again. If a valid option is entered, the goal succeeds and the entry is added to the database.

Arithmetical Operations

To do arithmetical operations, we use the same techniques of unification that have already been discussed. This is somewhat cumbersome, but remember that Prolog is not designed to support extensive numerical processing, no more than BASIC is designed to support formal reasoning.

To compute a sum, for example, create a predicate that binds a variable to the sum:

```
predicates
  plus(integer,integer,integer)
  displaysum(integer,integer)

clauses
  plus(X,Y,Sum) :-
    Sum=X+Y.

  displaysum(X,Y) :-
    plus(X,Y,Sum),
    write(Sum),nl.
```

The *plus* predicate forces the binding of *Sum,* returning the value to *displaysum.* This same method can be used with any type of arithmetical operation. Remember that *plus* is not a built-in predicate.

If desired, the equation expression could be used in the *displaysum* predicate:

```
displaysum(X,Y) :-
  Sum=X+Y,
  write(Sum),nl.
```

Again, remember that *Sum* must be a free variable. If *Sum* is a bound variable, $Sum = X + Y$ returns the value of *True* if *Sum* is bound to the total of *X* and *Y,* and returns the value of *False* if *Sum* is bound to any other value.

You can also use any of Turbo Prolog's functions as part of the expression:

```
displaysqrt(Y) :-
  Xsqrt=sqrt(Y),
  write(Xsqrt),nl.
```

The complete list of Turbo Prolog functions is shown in table 10.2.

Table 10.2
Turbo Prolog Arithmetical and Logical Predicate Functions

Predicate	Function
Arithmetical Operators	
X mod Y	remainder of X divided by Y
X div Y	quotient of X divided by Y
abs(X)	absolute value of X
cos(X)	cosine of X (radians)
sin(X)	sine of X (radians)
tan(X)	tangent of X (radians)
arctan(X)	arctangent of X
exp(X)	*e* raised to X
ln(X)	log to the base *e*
log(X)	log to the base 10
sqrt(X)	square root of X
random(X)	binds X to random number
round(X)	rounds X
Logical Predicates	
bitand(X,Y,Z)	bitwise AND (Z is result)
bitor(X,Y,Z)	bitwise OR
bitnot(X,Z)	bitwise NOT
bitxor(X,Y,Z)	bitwise exclusive OR
bitleft(X,N,Y)	bitwise shift *N* bits left
bitright(X,N,Y)	bitwise shift *N* bits right

When using functions, be sure to permit all input values that could be expected. For example, the following predicate raises a base to a real, positive, or negative exponent:

```
raise(_,Power,Result) :-
  Power=0,
  Result=1.0.

raise(Base,Power,Result) :-
  Power<0,
  X=0.0-Power,
  raise(Base,X,Temp),
  Result=1/Temp.

raise(Base,Power,Result) :-
  Power>0,
  Result=exp(Power*ln(Base)).
```

The clauses must ensure that all possible conditions are tested.

Delay Loops

There may be occasions when you need to place a delay loop in a Prolog program. An example could be the initial screen in which you display the title, information about your company, and then a copyright notice (and perhaps some graphics or animation). The initial screen is displayed for a short time before the screen is cleared and the program begins.

This can be accomplished with a *delay* predicate:

```
delay(0) :- !.
delay(N) :- NN=N-1, delay(NN).
```

Exercises

1. Write a logon routine for the automotive diagnostic system presented in chapter 7. Use recursion to permit retry up to three times before the program stops. The user should enter a name and ID number, which are compared against a list of facts (*names,ids*) in the static database.

2. For the same program in chapter 7, add an introductory display screen that displays a title for about ten seconds. What value did you use as the delay argument?

chapter $\boxed{11}$

Developing Programs with Turbo Prolog

□ Turbo Prolog has several features that are unique to Prolog as well as variations of standard features. Let's look at how these apply to program development.

Debugging Programs

It would be nice if programs always worked right the first time they are tried, but this is seldom the case. If you do have problems with a program's execution, Turbo Prolog includes a few tools to help you with debugging.

Trace

You can trace the execution of your program using either the *shorttrace* or *trace* compiler directive. The directive is placed near the beginning of the program:

```
shorttrace
database
  xpositive(symbol)
  xnegative(symbol)
```

```
predicates
  run
  diagnosed(symbol)
```

When the program is compiled and executed, the execution runs in single-step mode. The program pauses at each step until the user presses the F10 key. The trace window displays information about the execution as it progresses.

If possible, you should use the *shorttrace* compiler directive instead of *trace*. Turbo Prolog normally uses some optimization techniques to improve program execution speed and minimize memory requirements. The *trace* directive doesn't permit this optimization, but the *shorttrace* directive does. You will get less information in the trace window, but there is still enough to see what is happening.

If you do not want to trace the execution of the entire program, you can use a *trace(on)* standard predicate to control the starting point and *trace(off)* to control the terminating point. This permits you to examine a small part of the program without single stepping through the entire execution.

When using the *trace* predicates, two precautions should be observed:

1. You still need the *trace* or *shorttrace* compiler directive at the beginning of the program.
2. The starting point defaults to *trace(on)*. To trace part of the program, you will need a *trace(off)* near the beginning of the program, then a *trace(on)* where you want to start the trace.

Using the Save Predicate

Another alternative for tracing is to save the database at the end of the program:

```
run: -
  diagnosed(_),save"test.dat",clear_facts.
```

The *test.dat* database file will be, effectively, a trace of the program during execution, and should show the conclusions reached and the order in which they are reached. After the execution terminates, you can examine this file as you can any other Prolog program to see what was actually proven.

Determinism

You can use the *diagnostics* and *check_determ* compiler directives to find *nondeterministic* predicates. A nondeterministic clause is a clause that is capable of generating multiple solutions through backtracking. You can use the *diagnostics* predicate to display the names of the predicates used and certain basic information about each predicate. The display will show whether the predicate is deterministic or nondeterministic (see figure 11.1). You can use the *check__determ* compiler directive to find out more information.

```
  Run   Compile   Edit   Options   Files   Setup   Quit


┌──────────────────────── Diagnostics ────────────────────────┐


Predicate Name  Dbase Determ Size  Doml -- flowpattern
--------------  ----- ------ -----  -----------------------
goal            NO    YES      84   --
xpositive       YES   NO      103   symbol -- i
xnegative       YES   NO      103   symbol -- i
run             NO    YES     122   --
diagnosed       NO    NO     1353   symbol -- o
check           NO    YES     425   symbol -- i
positive        NO    YES     158   string,symbol -- i,i
negative        NO    YES     158   string,symbol -- i,i
clear_facts     NO    YES     142   --
remember        NO    YES     117   symbol,char -- i,i
ask             NO    YES      96   string,symbol,char -- i,i,o
--------------  ----- ------ -----  -----------------------
Total size              2861


Press the SPACE bar
```

F8:Previous line   F9:Edit   S-F9:View windows   S-F10:Resize window   Esc:Stop exec

Figure 11.1
Display of diagnostic output

The *repeat* predicate, for example, is always nondeterministic by design. In writing Prolog programs, you will normally use the cut to eliminate nondeterministic clauses and improve program efficiency.

Using the *diagnostics* and *check__determ* compiler directives permits you to identify nondeterministic predicates and decide where your cuts should be placed. In some cases, it will identify rules that are in error.

Building Libraries

As you progress in designing your expert systems, you will find that some of the same predicates (such as the *repeat* predicate) are used in many of your programs. Rather than writing them into your program each time, you can put these in a separate file and include them at compile time with the *include* directive:

```
include "prolog.lib"
```

The library file must follow the rules of Turbo Prolog program structures (with the appropriate sections), but you can define the predicates for the included clauses and the domains in the include file. You can place the *include* directive at any point in the program that represents a natural boundary (i.e., at the beginning of the program or between any two sections). Each included file should have its own domains, predicates, and clauses sections.

Using library files, as opposed to putting the predicates in the main program, will cause some loss of efficiency during compiling. But, in most cases, a special predicate file is a very valuable asset in designing expert systems. Eventually, you can create some very high-level predicates that simplify the design of complex systems. For example, you could define a *why* predicate for computer-generated explanations of how a goal is being calculated, an *ask* predicate for questions, or special input and output predicates for graphics or other features.

Using a Goal Section

When you compile a program to execute as a standalone program, a goal must be specified and defined as a section in your program. This goal section is normally placed after the predicates section. A compiled program will stop after the goal has succeeded once. If you want to see all solutions, use recursion and the *fail* predicate to force backtracking to solve the goal again.

Exercises

1. Add a goal section to the automotive diagnostic system of chapter 7. Compile it to execute as a standalone program.

2. Suppose there are two or more solutions in the diagnostic program. Modify the program to display all solutions when compiled for internal execution.

3. Modify the program to display all solutions when executing as a standalone program (compiled for external execution).

4. Use the *diagnostics* directive in the automotive diagnostic program in example 3. Print out the display and describe the meaning of each column.

part 2

Expert System Design

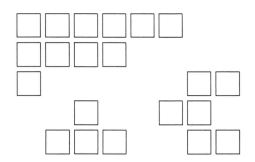

chapter 12

The Expert System

☐ Expert systems are computer programs that use inference techniques—which involve formal reasoning and normally require the expertise of a human expert—to solve problems in a specific domain. Expert systems are often a cost-effective alternative if the knowledge base is too large for a human expert to manage or the human expert is not available or too expensive.

Knowledge and Expert Systems

The term *expert system* originally was used to refer to a computer system that could perform at, or near, the level of a human expert. Today, an expert system is more formally defined as a computer program that uses knowledge and inference procedures to solve problems that are usually solved using human expertise.

The development of expert systems is considered part of a computer science referred to as artificial intelligence. However, expert systems are only intelligent in the sense that they model (rather than mimic) the thinking of an expert. The human expert must exist first. Development of an expert system involves codifying the problem-solving process of the human expert into an objective form. As such, the expert system only presents a limited extension of the expert's problem-solving process. There is no real "intelligence," nor is the expert system a substitute for the human expert.

Most expert systems could, perhaps, be more accurately called *knowledge systems*. This implies that the expert system can store a large base of facts (or knowledge) about a specific domain, the relationships of these facts, and the rules about how these facts can be used to solve problems. This collection of facts is said to be the *knowledge base*. The expert system can be used to solve problems when no defined procedure exists, because it can use its internal rules in the knowledge base to formulate a procedure.

The media prefers the term *expert systems*. Many software products for personal computers are said to employ "expert system techniques" or "artificial intelligence concepts" to improve the user interface or to approach new problems that have not previously been solved using personal computers. In most cases, the terminology is simply used to sell the program, and has little relationship to what we will discuss in the next few chapters. As a result, the term *expert systems* has come to have little meaning for most computer users.

The science of expert systems is still new, with the first productive systems dating from the early seventies. Unlike other areas of computer science, many terms have no standard definitions and theories are still changing. There is much, much room for creativity and discovery by today's knowledge engineers.

Characteristics of Expert System Tasks

Expert systems are best at applications that involve diagnostics, troubleshooting, analyzing, predicting, complex monitoring and control, interpreting, planning, learning, tutoring, natural language processing, and symbolic processing. They are used in applications where the procedures or algorithms for the problem are nonexistent or poorly defined (unstructured), but good heuristics do exist. Although their primary function today is as a tool for human experts, expert systems are rapidly being accepted for use by the nonexpert to solve problems when human expertise is expensive or unavailable.

If you are trying to make a decision about whether or not to develop an expert system to solve problems in a specific domain, use the following guidelines:

- the problem solution involves many possible goal states
- the problem solution requires formal reasoning
- no defined procedure exists
- the knowledge used for making the decision is dynamic
- the knowledge used for making the decision is uncertain
- experts cannot agree

Let's look at each of these characteristics of expert systems tasks in more depth.

The Problem Solution Involves Many Possible Goal States

If the problem has many possible goal states and it is impossible to examine each, consider using an expert system. A program to play chess, for example, must examine many possible alternatives for each move. There is no one "winning goal," but any of many possible goal states could win the game.

The Problem Solution Requires Formal Reasoning

The solution to the problem involves formal reasoning (inference and deduction) and symbolic processing with heuristics, rather than numerical processing with defined procedures.

No Defined Procedure Exists

If there is no defined procedure for solving the problem, it is impossible to solve it using the methods of traditional numerical processing. An expert system can develop its own procedure for the problem solution using what it knows about the domain.

Imagine a detective with many clues about a crime. All of these are facts that can be expressed using a symbolic language (for example, the suspect is over six feet tall). An expert system can work through the facts, selecting only what is relevant and reaching a conclusion based on what is known about the crime.

The Knowledge Used for Making the Decision Is Dynamic

If the knowledge used to define the procedure is constantly changing, with procedural languages it will be necessary to constantly modify the program based on the changing procedure. Expert systems permit the development of dynamic knowledge bases; the eventual procedures used to solve the problem created by the program at execution time use the dynamic knowledge in the knowledge base.

For example, the knowledge an engineer might use to configure a computer system would probably be very dynamic. The parts list—as well as the rules about what parts are needed for a specific application and how the parts work together—would be constantly changing. Even a good engineer would have a difficult time keeping track of all the cables, peripherals, adapter cards, and manuals needed for a minicomputer, mainframe, and even a microcomputer system. Using an expert system enables an engineer to keep track of the configuration rules as well as the parts that apply for any system.

The Knowledge About the Domain Is Uncertain

Expert systems can also function with uncertain knowledge. If the rules are uncertain, or if the input data is uncertain, or if the eventual goal state is uncertain, the system will still function usefully.

In medical diagnostic systems, certain symptoms may indicate a specific disease, but the input data may be uncertain. A child, for example, may have difficulty describing an acute abdominal pain, and a baby cannot describe any symptoms. Sometimes a symptom is readily apparent; sometimes it is masked by other symptoms. Some types of tests do not give conclusive results. Even if all the facts are correct, the conclusion may not be certain. Expert systems can still function in this type of environment.

The Experts Cannot Agree

In many domains, experts may disagree. It is still possible, however, to abstract the knowledge of each of them and combine these into a single expert system. The system can then be used to solve problems that eluded the individual experts and to identify contradictions in the knowledge base. (PROSPECTOR found an ore deposit that eluded nine experts.) Formulating an expert system when the experts disagree requires an objective abstraction. An expert system to display a horoscope would be quite another problem. The experts do not agree, and you would have a difficult time defining an objective domain.

Applications for Personal Computer Expert Systems

Some of the specific applications for expert systems on a personal computer include:

- configuring small computer systems
- analyzing alternative long-distance telephone services for a specific application
- diagnosing problems in computers, automobiles, video recorders, or other equipment
- analyzing corporate expense accounts for reimbursement
- forecasting local weather
- making operational decisions in a corporate environment
- analyzing food allergies and diagnosing diseases in small domains
- making tax strategy and investment decisions
- home or office monitoring and control (for example, fire, burglary, heating, and cooling)

Many applications that currently require a large computer system can be run on a personal computer if the domain is made smaller and more specific. For example, medical diagnostics require a very large computer. MYCIN and PUFF address specific and smaller domains in medical diagnostics. Smaller domains, perhaps addressing specific diseases, could easily be implemented on today's personal computers. As new information about the disease becomes available, it would be very easy to update the knowledge of the smaller system.

In the same way, nutritional analysis is probably too large a domain for a personal computer. An expert system to diagnose food allergies, however, might be quite within the range of a personal computer.

Limitations of Expert Systems

The biggest problem in building most expert systems is not developing the program, but distilling the information from the experts into a codified form that can be represented in the expert system. Human experts apply analogy, procedural analysis, formal reasoning, intuition, and common sense in the solution of problems. When the knowledge engineer begins a dialog with an expert in the process of designing a system, the engineer discovers that the human expert uses a rather subjective process that involves many techniques (see figure 12.1). The human expert has a very difficult time describing in an objective way how any particular problem is solved.

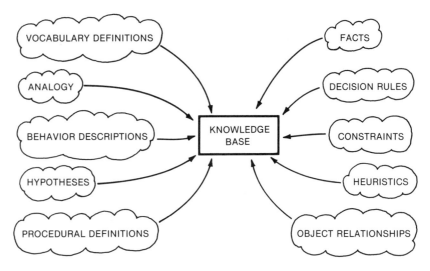

Figure 12.1
The human expert knowledge base

The knowledge engineer has no general theory that can be applied to all domains. The system development is more cyclic or based on trial-and-error, beginning with small prototypes and gradually expanding the system as the confidence of both the expert and knowledge engineer grows.

The expert system is limited to formal reasoning and occasionally to procedural analysis. The knowledge engineer's primary problems are analyzing how the expert approaches problems within the specific domain and defining this process in a form that can be implemented by an objective expert system.

Following are a few other limitations of expert systems that are important.

1. With most systems, the entire knowledge base must fit in the computer's memory. With many systems, it is possible to use disk storage to extend the database size, but the program will slow down dramatically unless a RAMdisk or similar device is used. Even with a RAMdisk, the system may still be too slow with large knowledge bases. Most of today's personal computer systems are limited to less than a thousand rules and a few hundred goal states. A good expert system for career counseling would need to support 60,000 goal states (possible occupations)—quite beyond the range of today's technology.

2. Expert systems cannot be used where there is limited knowledge or no knowledge (such as parapsychology).

3. Expert systems primarily use formal reasoning and limited numerical processing. Do not expect them to use analogy, intuition, or common sense. A dog has more common sense than any expert system. For this reason, expert systems do poorly when used for mathematical applications or perceptual problems.

4. Expert systems cannot access knowledge outside their domain of expertise. When approaching the edge of his or her expertise, a human expert's ability to solve problems degrades gracefully. In contrast, when an expert system approaches its edge of expertise, its ability degrades rapidly.

Advantages of Expert Systems

The expert system has the following advantages over the human expert:

- Expert systems can be used to solve problems when no procedure exists and the problem is very unstructured.
- Expert systems are often cost effective when human expertise is very expensive, not available, or contradictory.
- Expert systems can apply a systematic reasoning process with a very large knowledge base that is often much larger than a human expert can retain or utilize.
- The expert system is objective. It is not biased or prejudiced to a predetermined goal state, and it does not jump to conclusions.

- Expert systems are not influenced by perceptions that are not relevant. The human expert's decision is easily influenced by knowledge and perceptions not directly related to the problem. A politician is influenced by the lobbyist, a doctor by financial pressure, a corporate manager by personality conflicts with other managers. The expert system's decision is related strictly to the knowledge in the knowledge base.

Exercises

1. Identify a domain in which you consider yourself an expert. Could decisions in this domain be modeled by an expert system? Why or why not?

2. List several novel applications for an expert system on a personal computer using Turbo Prolog. Approximate the number of final goal states you would need for each application and the total number of rules you would expect to implement.

3. How would you distinguish between an expert system and a knowledge system?

chapter 13

Types of Knowledge Representation

☐ The knowledge engineer builds a model of a domain. From the model, the expert system is designed. The model is an abstraction of the domain as viewed by the expert. This chapter examines several methods of representing this knowledge. The method of knowledge representation eventually determines the type of expert system architecture (see chapter 14) that will be used.

Knowledge Representation

In any type of expert system, one key issue is how knowledge will be represented. Let's look for a moment at these knowledge representation concepts.

The basic unit of knowledge in the expert system is the *object*. This is a physical or conceptual entity that represents a real-world entity, such as *cat*, *car*, *john*, or *computer*. For the moment, we must distinguish between the type of object we refer to in this chapter and the Prolog object mentioned in the first part of this book.

The Prolog object (as defined in the Turbo Prolog manual) is often called an *atom* or *element* in other Prolog texts. The Prolog object is part of the Prolog language, and is a symbolic constant that can be used to represent real-world objects (physical or conceptual), properties or attributes of these objects, or the values of the properties or attributes. We could say that the Prolog object is part of any symbolic language. In previous chapters it was referred to as a symbolic object, but it is more properly called a language object.

In this chapter, the term *object* has nothing to do with any particular language; it can be implemented with any of several languages (including C or Pascal). This object, as well as other concepts to be introduced, is a theoretical concept.

The knowledge engineer models the abstraction of reality as seen by the expert. The knowledge engineer, then, is working at several levels of abstraction, as shown in figure 13.1. The first level is the real world, and the second is the abstraction of the expert. The expert tries to communicate knowledge to the knowledge engineer, who then forms a third-level abstraction that is called the knowledge representation. This knowledge representation contains objects, properties (attributes), and values. From this, the engineer abstracts again to a language with language objects (atoms, elements). This chapter examines the basic concepts of representing knowledge.

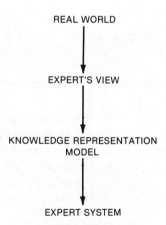

Figure 13.1
Levels of abstraction

One basic concept of any knowledge representation is *chunking*. Although chunks are a subjective phenomena, they are very important as the elementary pattern in perception and thinking. A chunk is a collection of knowledge stored and retrieved as a single unit. The human mind can process approximately seven chunks at one time. (Local telephone numbers, for example, contain only seven digits. If they contained more, they would be far more difficult to remember.) Single-processor computers normally process only one chunk at a time. Chunks are learned distinctions that people use to make high-level decisions. The human expert is distinguished from the nonexpert by his or her chunking ability in a specific domain. Any knowledge representation must take the basic concepts of objects, relationships, and chunks into account.

Knowledge can be expressed in many ways. In a typical system you may have facts, rules (relationships between facts), and taxonomies (relationships between objects). The type of representation used depends upon the type of knowledge that will be used by the expert system to make decisions.

Semantic Networks

Probably the oldest form of knowledge representation (and also the most general) is the semantic network. In this scheme the domain is represented by a collection of *nodes* and *links*. See figure 13.2.

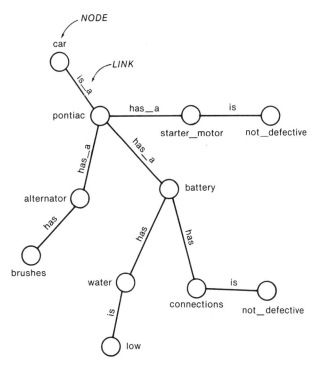

Figure 13.2
Semantic network

Although there are no specific conventions for naming nodes and links, the following rules apply in general.

1. Objects and descriptions about the objects are represented by nodes.

2. Relationships between objects or between objects and their descriptors are represented by links.

Certain types of links (relationships) are so common that they are given a special type of name.

121

The *is__a* relationship (link) is used to indicate that an object is a member of a larger class, for example, *pine is__a tree, the cat is__a Abyssinian,* or *Holmes is__a detective.* This type of link is used to express a taxonomic relationship. In Prolog, these facts could be expressed as:

```
is_a(pine,tree).
is_a(cat,abyssinian).
is_a(Holmes,detective).
```

The *has__a* relationship (link) is used to identify nodes that are the properties or attributes of objects (other nodes), for example, *the car has__a starter motor, the computer has__a disk drive,* or *the cat has__a color.*

```
has_a(car,starter_motor).
has_a(computer,disk_drive).
has_a(cat,color).
```

Definitional relationships are used to define values for attributes, for example, *the starter motor is defective, the color is ruddy,* or *the disk drive does turn.*

```
is(starter_motor,defective).
is(color,ruddy).
status(drive,turns).
```

Other links can be used to express causal relationships, for example, *a defective starter motor is caused by worn brushes.* The semantic network is very flexible, and is often the first tool used by the knowledge engineer when trying to represent a domain.

Another very important aspect of the semantic network is that it can express *inheritance.* Inheritance refers to the ability of one node to assume the characteristics of another node. More specifically, all members of a class are assumed to have the properties of a more general class of which they are a part.

For example, if a pine is a tree and trees have leaves, we can assume the pine has leaves. Nodes at a lower level in the network inherit characteristics of nodes at a higher level. If cats have four legs and an Abyssinian is a cat, then an Abyssinian has four legs.

Object-Attribute-Value Triplets

Factual knowledge can be represented as a table of *object-attribute-value* (O-A-V) triplets. Each object has one or more properties or attributes, and each attribute has a value.

Object	Attribute	Value
car	starter_motor	defective
car	battery_water	good
car	battery_connections	good
abyssinian	color	ruddy
disk_drive_motor	status	turns

When we start a consultation session with an expert system, the values of the goal state attributes are unknown. As you progress through the consultation, the expert system obtains values for the attributes at intermediate goal states, eventually determining the values for the attributes at the final goal state. Factual knowledge is expressed in the system as object-attribute-value triplets.

In comparison with the semantic network, we can see that the O-A-V triplet table is a special case of the semantic network's nodes and links. Objects, attributes, and values are the semantic network's nodes. The object-attribute relationship is the same as the *has_a* link and the attribute-value relationship is the same as the definitional link. By comparing the examples in these two sections, this will be clearer.

In a simple knowledge representation, you may use attribute-value pairs (A-V pairs) instead of triplets. In such a system the domain has a single object and inheritance (see the section in this chapter on frame representation) cannot be represented.

Rule Representation

Triplets and pairs can be used to represent facts, but we may also want to represent relationships between facts. Rules express relationships between O-A-V triplets or A-V pairs.

IF the starter motor turns with a grinding sound

AND the battery voltage is good

THEN the starter motor is defective.

Each rule has a conclusion and an antecedent. If all the conditions of the antecedent are true (each premise), the conclusion must be true.

It is also possible to use variables in rules. In this way you can use a single rule to represent several relationships by simply binding the variable before the rule is used. For example:

IF the cost of stock X is dropping

AND the cost of stock X has dropped below Y

THEN purchase Z shares of stock X.

If facts and relationships are uncertain, rules can be used to express conclusions and the certainty of the calculated conclusions (explained in chapter 19).

123

All rules are basically operators, providing a technique for moving the system from one state to another. Simple rules that relate facts are called *production rules,* and are the basis of the rule-based expert system (see chapter 14). *Metarules* are rules about other rules. Metarules are useful for defining heuristics, or problem-solving strategies.

In a particular rule representation, rules can be static or dynamic. In a static representation, the rules in the domain remain fixed and are not changed during the consultation. In a dynamic representation, the rules can change.

Rule-based representation is probably closest to the way a human expert approaches a problem solution. If you observe a skilled human's behavior on poorly structured tasks, the person often appears to know what to do at each step. He or she seems to behave as if there were a large number of rules, each of which associates some particular action with a set of conditions under which that action is appropriate. If you ask why a task was performed a certain way, the expert will be able to identify a number of features of the situation that acted as a signal for the specified action. The rule is a basic chunk in this type of representation.

Expert systems that use rules are known as production systems. We will discuss the production system in more depth in the next chapter.

Frame Representation

A frame-based representation is a representation in which the basic storage unit is the *concept.* A concept is a collection of physical or conceptual entities of the same class. A concept is represented by a *frame.*

The frames are arranged in a hierarchy, with some concepts (frames) "belonging to," or subclasses of, other frames. The taxonomy looks much like an inverted tree, with the frames at different levels (see figure 13.3). If a frame at a lower level is linked to a frame at a higher level, the lower-level frame is said to *inherit* the characteristics of the higher-level frame. For example, if trees have limbs and a pine is a tree, a pine also has limbs. A frame at one level is the *parent* of any frame that inherits its characteristics. The inheriting frame is the *child.*

There are two types of concepts, or frames. A *primitive concept* is a frame that has no parent. Primitive concepts are the highest level frames in the system; they have guidelines, but no absolute definitions can be given. If the frame does have a parent, it is a *definitional concept.* Definitional concepts can be defined in terms of primitive concepts and other definitional concepts. In this example, *tree* is a primitive concept. All the other concepts are definitional.

Concepts can have properties (attributes) and roles. A *property* is a specific quality of a concept. Properties have values:

Concept	Property	Value
The car	color is	blue.

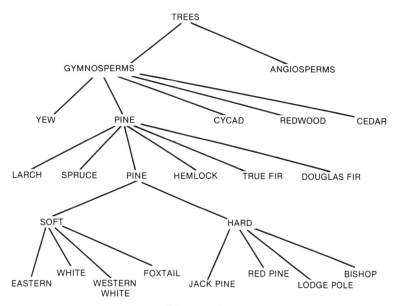

Figure 13.3
A collection of frames showing hierarchy

The values can be numeric (for example, floating point or integer) or a member of a set (for example, blue, red, or white). Values may also be restricted by limits.

Roles represent the components of a concept. Roles can also have values, which can also be numeric or a member of a set. Limits may also be imposed:

Concept	Role	Value
The battery	water is	low.

Whether a given entity is a property or a role depends upon the context or domain representation. If a given property does not support the level of detail needed, make it a role. Conversely, if a role describes something in too much detail, make it a property.

In a frame, the various attributes and roles for a concept are represented by filler slots in the frame. An example of a frame representation is shown in figure 13.4. Each slot can contain a value for an attribute or a role. If the value must be determined dynamically when the program is executed, the slot can contain either a production rule or a procedure for evaluating a value. It is even possible for a slot to contain multiple values, such as a list (set of ordered values). An example of a slot for multiple values might be a slot containing the names of two or more brothers.

Some slots, called *facets,* may be used to define constraints for other slots, such as a minimum or maximum value or the maximum number of values for a list in another slot.

When a slot value needs to be evaluated for a slot, the procedure or

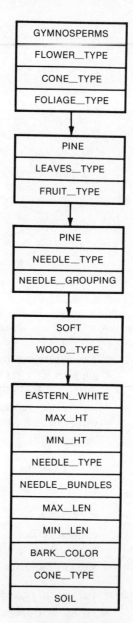

Figure 13.4
A frame representation

production rules for that slot are activated. If it is a procedure, it is said to be an *attached procedure*. Procedures or production rules for a slot are activated when they become a subgoal for another goal.

In a given representation, frames may be static or dynamic. In a static system, the relationships and contents of the frames are static during any particular consultation. In a dynamic system, the relationships and contents can change.

Frame representation has several advantages over other forms. For this reason, it has enjoyed a growing popularity in many of the better expert systems. For example:

1. Both declarative and procedural methods can be used to evaluate a value. When a procedure is the most efficient way to calculate a value, a procedure is used. When a procedure does not exist or is not explicit, declarative methods can be used.

2. Anything can be stored in a filler slot. You can even store graphic procedures in a slot. For example, if a computer diagnostic routine needs to show the location of a bad memory chip or where to measure a voltage on a board, the graphic procedure can be stored in the appropriate slot to display where a chip is located or where to measure the voltage.

3. Frames enable the knowledge engineer to easily visualize the relationships and the hierarchy of the domain.

The primary disadvantages of the frame system are the increased complexity of the rule system and the difficulty of expressing exceptions in a particular inheritance. For example, if all members of a particular tree family had leaves except one, how could you indicate that all members exept one inherit this characteristic?

Frames are most appropriate when there is a hierarchy in the knowledge base and this hierarchy is fairly static. If the domain does not have a hierarchy (it is *flat*), frame systems may not offer a significant advantage.

Other Representations

This chapter has reviewed semantic networks, object-attribute-value triplets, rule-based representations, and frame-type representations as the primary representation schemes. But other schemes, such as first-order logic representations, are also available. In all cases, the goal of the knowledge engineer is to find the most accurate representation to model the given domain. After this is accomplished, the engineer must locate the best language to implement the representation.

Exercises

1. Give an example of what might be represented as a flat domain. Why do you consider it a flat domain?

2. The automotive diagnostic system was created as a rule-based system. Can you create a frame representation of a similar system? If so, how would this be written in Prolog?

chapter $\boxed{14}$

Types of Expert Systems

☐ Most Prolog expert systems are one of two types: production or frame. This is generally referred to as the *architecture* of the system. Let's look at both of these systems.

The Production System

The most common type of expert system is the *production system*. In a production system, the knowledge is rule based and stored as a collection of IF-THEN rules. Each rule is said to be a *production rule*. The rules express relationships between facts. The facts are expressed as O-A-V triplets or A-V pairs.

The basic components of a production system are *working memory,* a *rule base,* and an *inference engine* (see figure 14.1). The working memory and rule base together are called the *knowledge base*. Sometimes a system may include additional components such as an explanatory interface, a natural language interface, or a knowledge acquisition system.

The Rule Base

The basic knowledge concerning the relationships of facts about the domain are stored as a rule base in a series of IF-THEN rules, which are

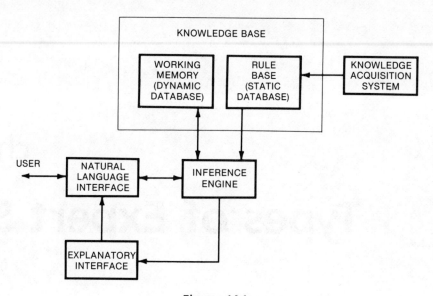

Figure 14.1
The production system

the production rules. These are represented as clauses in a Prolog program, and are stored in static memory. The static memory, then, is the rule base.

A typical production system might be:

```
diagnosed(starter_motor) if
  not(check(engine_turns_over)) and
  check(electrical_power) and
  check(relay) and
  not(check(starter_motor)).
```

This can be read as:

> IF the engine does not turn over
>
> AND electrical power is at the starter motor
>
> AND the starter motor relay pulls in
>
> AND the starter motor does not turn properly
>
> THEN the starter motor is probably defective.

Notice that the rule expresses a relationship between O-A-V triplets, with the goal state defining the attribute value of an object.

There may be hundreds of rules in the rule base of a typical expert system, and these form the basis of the formal reasoning process that the system uses to solve a problem. Most of the expert system program consists of these rules. The rules form a hierarchical structure, approaching the problem from the general to the specific in a symptomatic approach.

In any given production system, there are three types of rules or productions.

1. Facts about the domain. For example, if the alternator has brushes, we could express this as:

```
has(alternator,brushes).
```

Most of the facts in a production rule base (i.e., static database in a Prolog program) are used to express the taxonomy of the domain, or the relationship between objects.

2. The relationship between facts. For example:

```
diagnosed(starter_motor) if
  not(check(engine_turns_over)) and
  check(electrical_power) and
  check(relay) and
  not(check(starter_motor)).
```

3. Heuristics, or rules that are used to control the reasoning process. For example, we might use a rule to ask a multichoice question, using the answer to determine which rules to pursue next.

As mentioned in chapter 5, the first part of the Prolog rule is called the head, consequence, or conclusion. The second part consists of a series of conclusions and is the tail, or antecedent. The antecedent consists of one or more *premises* or conditions. The antecedent represents a *pattern* and the rule is said to be triggered if each condition (premise or goal) in the antecedent is found to be true. The conclusion is then said to be *True* and the rule is said to *fire*. This conclusion, then, is saved and can be used with the facts to fire other rules. Each conclusion is, essentially, an intermediate goal state or node in the search space.

Working Memory

Working memory contains facts that describe what is known about a particular problem. Dynamic memory is the working memory in a Prolog program.

When a program is started, working memory is empty and contains no knowledge. As the consultation progresses and the system learns more about the problem, the new knowledge is put into working memory. The knowledge in working memory is used to fire additional rules. As each rule fires, the conclusion is added to working memory with the facts already known.

There are several ways of using working memory effectively, depending upon the type of expert system (for example, diagnostic or predictive) and the domain. In the most general case, working memory is used to store facts from the user and conclusions (goals) as they are proven true or false. You may even want to use two databases in working memory: one for facts and goals that are proven true and one for facts and goals that are proven false. For example, if the engine turns over, then *engine__turns__over* would be stored in working memory for true goals; if it does not turn over, the fact would be stored in working memory for false goals.

The program queries the user, finding out information and adding the knowledge to working memory. Facts in the database are used to trigger and fire additional rules, after which the conclusions are added to working memory.

Systems can be either static (monotonic) or dynamic (non-monotonic). In a static system, after a fact is added to working memory during the consultation it cannot be removed until the end of the consultation. If a goal is proven true or false and added to working memory, it cannot be removed from working memory during the consultation. When the next consultation starts, working memory will be empty again. In other words, attribute values cannot change during a consultation.

In a dynamic system, the facts and goals stored in working memory can change during the consultation (attribute values can change). If a fact in working memory changes, this can also affect the firing of particular rules. Conclusions become undone, and there must be a way to retrace and undo other facts that change with the conclusion, removing additional conclusions from working memory as necessary.

The Inference Engine

The inference engine (also called the rule interpreter) performs two tasks: one is inference, and the second is control.

The Inference Component

The *inference component* uses the facts in working memory to try to trigger new rules. After all conditions of a rule are triggered, the rule fires and the conclusion is added to working memory. The inference operates by a rule called *modus ponens*. Modus ponens—the basis of all formal logic—states that if a rule exists such that "IF A, THEN B" and if A is known to be true, then B is true. If a premise is true, the resulting conclusion must be true.

Although this rule seems simple in principle, in reality the human brain is far more efficient at this type of symbolic processing. Words have variable meanings, depending upon how they are used. There are contextual meanings that depend upon culture and social conventions. An expression may mean one thing to one person, and quite a different thing to someone else. The computer, in contrast, is quite objective. The specific formal rules have "hard" meanings that are quite static.

The inference component must also deal with the following situations:

1. Certain input information may be missing. If the user cannot answer a question, the consultation must not stop (as in traditional program execution). The program must be able to move toward the goal

in another direction, backtracking as necessary and then moving forward again.

2. Certain information may not be known with certainty. For example, there may be a 60 percent certainty that a particular fact is true. Conclusions, in the same way, may not be certain conclusions. If all the facts are known for certain, there may only be an 80 percent certainty that the starter motor is bad, for example. If we had more facts, this may be higher. There may also be probabilities associated with facts and conclusions.

3. You may want to query how the expert system reached a specific conclusion. For example, if you took your child to a medical doctor and the doctor determined that your child had measles, you would want to know why the doctor reached this conclusion. In the same way, if a computerized expert system reaches the same conclusion, you would want to know why this conclusion was reached.

In a production system, all knowledge is expressed as rules or facts. If rules are included as part of the inference engine to control the reasoning process, these inference rules must be functionally separated from the production rules. This makes it possible to update the rule base without altering the inference engine. With Turbo Prolog, both types of rules are in the clauses section. Usually, you would want to put inference rules first, then the rule base.

The Control Component

The control component determines the order in which the rules are scanned. There are basically four phases of the control cycle:

1. Unification—the matching process to determine what matches the specified goal.
2. Conflict resolution or selection—if several rules contain conclusions that match the goal, there must be a way of determining which rule to test at a particular time. In an IBM PC XT with linear processing, only one rule can be tested at a time.
3. Firing—the actual firing of the rule, acknowledging the fact that all subgoals match the specified conditions.
4. Action—the conclusion is added to working memory.

An illustration of this cycle is shown in figure 14.2. Only one rule can fire in each cycle. If the facts in working memory unify with several rules, the control component must decide which rule to fire.

In our automotive repair example, when the goal *diagnosed(__)* is invoked, the system will discover many conclusions that unify with this goal. Prolog must have some way of determining which rule will be selected for testing. In some systems, more than one rule may meet the conditions of the specified goal. In that case, the control strategy must decide which of the rules will actually fire, adding only one conclusion a cycle to the database.

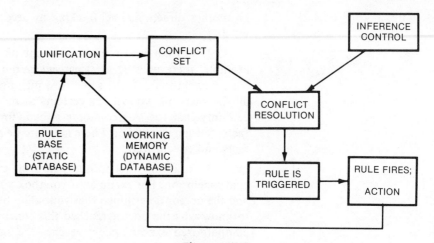

Figure 14.2
The production system control cycle

The control component has two decisions to make: what is the starting point, and how can the search be made more efficient. The starting point is the clause that will be tested first. The efficiency of the search is determined by the heuristics and the order in which the clauses are tested.

For Prolog, the starting point decision is simple. Prolog always starts by testing the first clause that matches the goal. In the automotive repair example, this will be *diagnosed(starter__motor)*. The search strategy is determined by the order of the clauses for the same predicate. Within a specific predicate, then, the order of the clauses in a Prolog program is very important because it determines the control flow (explained in the next chapter).

Auxiliary Production System Routines

A complete expert system normally has one or more auxiliary modules: a knowledge acquisition module, an explanatory interface, and a natural language interface.

The Knowledge Acquisition System

The knowledge acquisition system is used to add rules to the rule base or to edit existing rules. For most Prolog systems, this is nothing more than an editor. Turbo Prolog contains an internal editor that can be used to add or edit rules. The editor can also be accessed dynamically from a program as it is executing. In more sophisticated systems, this routine checks new, added rules for conflicts with existing rules.

The Natural Language Interface

An expert system, even in Prolog, uses a cryptic language that is difficult to read. Symbolic representations such as *starter__motor* are hardly the vocabulary of the user. Even the simplest expert system usually supports questions that can be answered by yes or no. More complex systems support multichoice questions and inputting attributes in response to questions, such as:

```
How many beeps do you hear when the machine is turned on?
```

The better expert systems permit the user to respond to questions in English sentences:

```
What seems to be the problem?
The car does not start.
```

The system would *parse* the answer to find the various parts of the response, using this to form a goal and to initiate the reasoning process. The expert system rules that are added to support this parsing and goal definition are the natural language interface.

The Explanatory Interface

You may want to respond to a question with "why," forcing the system to display the current reasoning chain. This is no different from a dialog with any expert. We do not always like to accept the conclusion of a complex chain of reasoning without asking for information about the reasoning process. Sherlock Holmes may provide the answer for a complex case, but you can always expect those around him to ask how he reached this conclusion. With an expert system, the rules and predicates used to support this input query are said to be the explanatory interface.

The Human Mind

The human mind functions much like a rule-based system, and includes both long-term memory and short-term memory. Short-term memory is much like a computer's memory, and stores information for only a short time (15-20 minutes). Long-term memory, in contrast, stores information throughout our life. Information in long-term memory is stored as patterns, continuously being accessed and used for "unifying" perceptions and conclusions already stored in short-term memory. Short-term memory is working memory, and long-term memory is the rule base.

The Frame System

Another type of expert system is the *frame system,* which (as you would imagine) is based on frame-type knowledge representation (see chapter 13). A typical production system may contain several hundred rules. As the complexity of the rule base increases, it becomes very difficult for the knowledge engineer to control the rule base. Rules added or edited may contradict other rules in the rule base. More important, the knowledge engineer loses a sense of the interaction between the rules. The hierarchical relationship of the rules is lost to the engineer.

It is possible to build frame-type systems with Prolog, and at least one version of Prolog (Arity) is available with additional built-in predicates to support frame-type expert systems. The majority of this book, however, focuses on production systems.

Other Systems

There are other types of expert systems, each of which offers advantages and disadvantages for the designer. The blackboard systems, for example, provide a common work area that is used by multiple processors, which can approach the problem using different knowledge representations and architectures.

Many systems are not specifically one type or another. For example, the Arity expert system is a frame-type Prolog system that also supports rules. You have a choice of using either—a large number of built-in predicates enable you to take advantage of the best of each type of architecture.

Summary

Expert systems are still a new science and there is much room for the development of new concepts of knowledge representation and the emergence of new types of expert system architectures. There is little in the way of a general science that can be applied to all domains. At present, a knowledge engineer cannot take a procedure or theory and use this to convert an expert's knowledge to a workable expert system.

Exercises

1. In the automotive diagnostic system, identify the inference engine, the rule base, and working memory.

2. What are the advantages and disadvantages of Prolog for the inference engine?

chapter 15

Search Strategies

□ An expert system may contain a large volume of knowledge. After we specify a goal that we want the system to solve, the expert system begins to apply its internal knowledge in finding the solution of that goal. The system, essentially, must define its own procedure for the problem.

There must be some order in this search, although there is no procedure stored that can define how the problem will be solved. There must be some implied strategy or procedure in how the system goes about using the rules (in a production system) and finding the final goal state (solving the problem).

The four basic strategies for defining the search procedure are forward reasoning, backward reasoning, heuristic reasoning, and decision trees. This chapter will look at each of these.

The Search Space

We could consider the matrix of goals and subgoals in an expert system as a *search space*. The starting point represents an initial node in the search space and the final goal represents the final node in the search space. In between are many nodes or subgoals (see figure 15.1). Like a frog moving from one lily pad to the next in a pond, the objective is to move from one subgoal to the next, eventually reaching the final goal.

Heuristics are strategies that enable you to move through the search space most efficiently, but there is no guarantee that a given path (or heuristic) will lead to the final goal or that it is the shortest path.

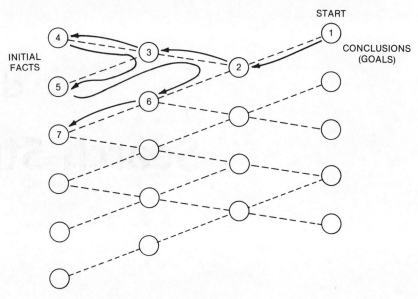

Figure 15.1
Prolog search strategy: backward chaining, depth first

With large search spaces, it is generally best to use hierarchical methods to reduce the search space. In a system in which each node in the search space has 10 branches, a 20-step search path would require 1020 trials. With a hierarchical search space, 90 percent of these are eliminated at the first node. Then 90 percent of the remaining paths are eliminated at the next node.

Imagine, for example, a medical diagnostic system and the number of possible symptoms that must be checked if a hierarchy is not used. This same system could be made far more manageable by grouping symptoms into classes to form a hierarchy. For example, you could ask if the patient has a cough. If the patient does have a cough, then you would use questions to find the type of cough (for example, light, hacking, or whooping). The symptom questions should work from the general to the specific.

Search-space searching is a generate and test process. The process has two parts. The first is generating all possible solutions that meet the specified goal. The second is testing and pruning solutions that fail to satisfy the specified constraints. A generator is said to be complete if it can produce all possible solutions. The generator is nonredundant if it produces each solution only once. The search generator should be complete and nonredundant.

For the design of efficient expert systems, the following should be true of the search space.

1. The knowledge and data should be reliable. The data should not be "noisy" (subject to random variations) or contain errors.

2. The knowledge and data should be static. This eliminates the need to reason with time-dependent variables or to retract facts or conclusions after they're proven true or false. This is not always completely possible. For example, a monitoring system must reason with sensor data, which often varies with time.

3. The search space should be small. The expert system knowledge base is stored in finite memory. The storage abilities of today's computers are still much, much smaller than the storage abilities of the human mind.

If it is necessary to work with large, complex problems using small expert systems, the strategy should be to partition the problem into several smaller problems. Design your expert system to resolve the smaller problems. In some cases, it may be necessary to factor the problem more than once. You can even design an expert system to reason your way through the factoring process. In factoring, you should start from the general and go to the specific, working top-down.

Backward and Forward Chaining

The two primary control strategies are backward chaining and forward chaining. Each of these, in turn, can also employ either depth-first or breadth-first strategies. Let's look at each of these.

Backward Chaining

In a backward-chaining system, a goal is assumed. The system works backward from the goal trying to prove it from the facts in the database or from knowledge supplied during the consultation. This strategy works reasonably well when the number of outcomes (final goal states) is relatively limited and the amount of input knowledge is very large. A possible goal (A-V pair or O-A-V triplet) is assumed and the program tries to prove it. If this fails, the next outcome (goal state) is assumed and the program tries to prove this. This continues until one of the goals is proven true. Backward-chaining systems are often called goal-directed systems.

The automotive diagnostic system in the first part of this book uses backward chaining. We begin by assuming a goal state (the starter motor is bad) and then try to prove this true. When this goal fails, the chaining reverses itself temporarily (forward chaining), finds another goal, and then tries to prove this new goal is true. This continues until a goal is proven true or all paths have been tested.

Backward-chaining systems are not efficient when the number of possible conclusions is very large. For example, imagine a career counseling system that supports hundreds of possible career decisions. Testing each goal would take a long time.

Forward Chaining

If the number of possible conclusions is large and the amount of input information is relatively small, forward chaining is more appropriate. In this case, premises of rules are examined against the information to see if the conclusions are true. If so, the conclusion is added to the database and the cycle repeats. As a result, forward-chaining systems are called data-driven systems.

Forward chaining is much like a detective working through a maze of clues to the final murder suspect. Without some level of forward reasoning, the number of suspects (final goal states) is very, very large. To reduce the number of possible suspects, the clues are examined and from this new conclusions are made. The suspect may be found to be a tall male from the account of a witness who saw him leave the scene. We might also conclude that the suspect wore an English tweed coat from a few threads pulled from the coat by the victim. These conclusions, in turn, are used to form new conclusions (fire additional rules). Eventually, we narrow the conclusions down to a single suspect and the crime is solved.

In another situation, the same detective may use backward reasoning. If the murder took place in a mansion and there were only twelve people at the mansion that evening, the detective may assume that each of these, in turn, is a suspect. The detective then tries to prove or disprove each of the twelve goal states, checking alibis. Forward chaining uses clues; backward chaining uses alibis.

> **Note:** If you have played the game *Whodunit,* you have discovered that you can win the game finding alibis or finding clues. The secret to winning the game is knowing when to use each.

Prolog and Chaining

The shape of the search space determines whether forward or backward chaining is best. If there is a lot of input information and few conclusions, backward chaining is best. If there is little input information and a lot of conclusions, forward chaining is best (see table 15.1).

Prolog systems are predominately backward-chaining systems with limited forward chaining. In our automotive diagnostic system, we start with one solution and work backward trying to prove it. If the hypothesis fails, Prolog goes forward until it can find the next hypothesis, then uses backward chaining again. Prolog can be used in forward-chaining systems, but it is most often used in backward-chaining systems.

Breadth-First Versus Depth-First Searching

In addition to distinguishing search strategies as forward or backward, search strategies can also be distinguished as depth first or breadth first. In a depth-first search, details are pursued as deeply as possible until the

Table 15.1
Comparison of Backward and Forward Chaining

Backward Chaining	Forward Chaining
Goal driven	Data driven
Starts from the possible solutions and works backward to see if one is correct	Starts from the data and works forward to see if a solution is consistent with the data
Starts by asking a question about a goal state	Starts from a situation and tries to respond
Can explain its reasoning	Does not explain its reasoning
Top-down reasoning	Bottom-up reasoning
Reduces search space by minimizing and structuring questions properly	Reduces search space by finding constraints to limit search

goal fails. In our automotive example, depth-first searching is used. Each possible outcome is pursued as deeply as possible using backward chaining until proven false. After an outcome is proven false, the system backs up and then pursues the next outcome.

In breadth-first searching, all possible conclusions at one level are pursued before moving to the next level. Breadth-first strategies are more efficient if the search starts with relatively few nodes, but at progressively deeper levels the number of nodes at a particular level rapidly increases.

As with the chaining strategy, the shape of the search space determines whether depth-first or breadth-first searching is most efficient. An expert system for chess playing, for example, would find breadth-first strategies far more efficient. The number of nodes at deeper levels becomes very, very large. Breadth-first searching enables you to eliminate many of the dead-end nodes very early in the search procedure.

For most applications, depth-first searching is preferred because it is closer to the way a human expert thinks. All details relative to a specific conclusion are considered together and either accepted or rejected.

Prolog always uses depth-first searching. This is either an advantage or disadvantage, depending upon the problem.

Prolog and Search Strategies

Prolog is considered a high-level language for symbolic processing. It is very good at supporting the design of expert systems, but the inference engine is internal to Prolog and provides little opportunity for user modification. This means the user does not have to spend time with inference engine programming, but it does limit the user to the search strategies that Prolog supports: that is, depth-first searching using backward chaining and limited forward chaining. This means Prolog is most efficient when used with specific search space shapes and becomes inefficient with other types. Prolog works best when the number of possible

141

final goal states is relatively small and the knowledge known about the problem is large.

Decision Tree Search Strategies

One basic philosophy in designing the search strategy is to ask the questions so that as much of the search space as possible is eliminated as quickly as possible. If you are using dialog questions with the first answer yes or no, either answer should eliminate approximately half of the possible search space. If you draw a map of the questions and the search flow, you should see a matrix that looks like an inverted tree. The matrix is the decision tree and represents the flow of the search strategy.

If the first question is a multichoice question with five possible answers, whatever answer the user selects should eliminate about 80 percent of the goal states. With one question, you have reduced your search space by 80 percent!

There is no rule, of course, that states you must order your rules and questions in this way. As you learn more about the domain, you can just add each of the rules to the rule base and the system would still work. Eventually, though, efficiency drops and the system becomes very slow. Decision tree structures improve efficiency by imposing some level of structure on the search, that is, a search space topology. As you design your expert systems, you will probably find it efficient to use some level of decision trees in your design.

Because decision trees impose a structure, they also imply a formal procedural level on the expert system. Many expert systems written in procedural languages utilize decision trees. For example, a user can define some examples of the relationship of certain data to eventual goal states, creating a decision tree. The system then compiles this to formal rules, identifying where knowledge is missing. The user can then "plug" these holes, eventually creating a consistent knowledge base.

The problem with such procedural expert systems is that the decision tree grows exponentially with the knowledge. There is a lot of duplication and the resulting system quickly becomes unmanageable and inefficient. In a true expert system, the size of the knowledge base grows linearly with the knowledge. There is little duplication and the relationship of the knowledge is easy to control. Decision trees can be used in good expert systems, but they should be used with the awareness that they impose a structure on the search strategy. The structure may be good or bad, depending upon the problem and the skill of the knowledge engineer.

Heuristic Search Strategies

There is one final search strategy that should be mentioned: the heuristic strategy. In this method, the formal rules define the eventual search strategy. The system looks at the knowledge available, then uses its own internal rules to define whether backward or forward reasoning is most appropriate and the order in which to search through the rules.

Exercises

1. What are some general methods of reducing the search space that could apply to several domains?

2. Which search strategy is best for:

    a. Planning

    b. Diagnostics

    c. Monitoring and control

chapter $\boxed{16}$

Defining the
Goal and Domain

☐ Now let's design a production-type expert system using Turbo Prolog. This chapter begins the process, starting with the design of an expert system that can be used to diagnose problems in IBM PC compatible computers.

Approaching the Problem

The human expert uses a variety of techniques to solve problems: numerical/procedural processing, analogy, formal reasoning, common sense, and intuition. The human mind is very adept at approaching a problem from many angles, comparing alternative problem-solving methods and using multiple techniques to reach the final goal. The human mind uses multiple strategies, parallel processing, and symbolic reasoning.

Imagine, for example, that you are sick and visit your doctor. You have a fever, your body aches, and you have chills. The doctor does a few tests and looks at the results (numerical processing), compares your symptoms and the test results with his medical knowledge (formal reasoning), and hypothesizes that you have the flu. The symptoms may not exactly match his medical knowledge, but if he treated someone with symptoms similar to yours for flu a few weeks ago and the patient got well, he may assume that you have the flu as well (analogy). In some cases, the doctor may observe unusual symptoms that do not match anything in his medical knowledge, but the doctor is able to make a diagnosis from an instinctive feeling based on a large reservoir of experience (intuition).

If you asked how the diagnosis was made, the doctor could tell you some of the reasoning process. But most of the techniques used were almost reflexive, without much thinking about the diagnostic process itself. The doctor recognized the problem and brought all of his resources to bear on the solution.

The human mind, in this sense, is a wonderful creation that has a processing power far beyond any computer man has created. When the knowledge engineer begins the dialog process with the doctor to build the expert system, the engineer is primarily trying to capture the formal reasoning process used by the doctor and perhaps a few procedural aspects. From this, the engineer tries to build a structured system from what is really a very subjective process. If a patient fails to respond, the doctor switches to another strategy, making a second diagnostic assumption. There may be allergic reactions to a medicine, forcing the doctor to try another alternative. There may be a multiple diagnosis.

In general, the human expert (doctor) does not use a linear process to solve the problem. The path to the solution is cyclic, moving forward toward the goal at times but retreating and trying another path at other times. There is no guarantee of a solution, and the human expert will normally use heuristics (rules of thumb) to reach a solution as quickly as possible.

The knowledge engineer has the extremely complex job of reducing this complex subjective process to an objective form, abstracting it to a formal knowledge representation, and then defining a set of formal rules that function with the skill of the human expert.

Let's use another example, career counseling. Interest tests can broaden our horizons to new job opportunities. An aptitude test can be used to determine our skills and abilities or where we lack skills and abilities. When the career counselor sits down with us and explores the decision in depth, however, we will probably find that the tests have little meaning. The counselor knows that many job definitions are changing rapidly. A secretary today, for example, must have quite different skills than one a few years ago. A corporate executive secretary will have a quite different job description than a secretary for a high school administrator. The tests do not adequately distinguish these differences, nor can they keep up with changing job descriptions.

The counselor dialogs with us, looking for nonverbal, as well as verbal, responses to questions. Do we want to live in the country or city? Do we enjoy traveling? What economic resources do we have for training? We will probably learn that there is no one goal or job toward which we should aim. For different vocations, there are trade-offs, disciplines that must be accepted, and rewards. Some jobs are more stressful than others. Can you imagine trying to capture all of this dialog process in an expert system?

Expert systems have been built, however, and many function effectively. Care should be taken to realize that because of their limitations they cannot replace the human expert. They can be used as tools by experts, helping them to work with large rule bases that are too complex for the human mind to manage.

The design of any expert system is a level of abstraction. The expert is dealing with a problem involving real-world entities. The real world is analog, with object attribute values that vary over an infinite spectrum. A specific flower is not red, nor is it carmine red. It is a real flower with a unique color; we have to use some level of abstraction to describe it.

The expert begins by forming a level of abstraction of the reality in his mind. The expert builds a miniature model of the problem with symbols representing the objects and discrete values representing the attributes. When the knowledge engineer attempts to build an expert system, the engineer builds a model of the model—another level of abstraction. The actual programming is yet another level of abstraction. In essence, the engineer is building a model of the process that the human expert is using to solve the problem.

The problem to be solved is basically unstructured, and will resist any type of systematic approach to its solution. Our only choice is how the abstraction will take place or how we will represent the knowledge. We can define the domain, the objects, and the object attributes of interest. We can then define the rules that specify relationships we know about objects and their attributes. The basic problem in expert system design is knowledge representation.

Defining the Goal

The first step is to define the specific goal the system is to achieve. The whole purpose of the expert system is to use a collection of knowledge to lead the user from point X to point Y. This cannot be accomplished unless the knowledge engineer has a clear knowledge of where point Y is located. The goal needs to be stated in a clear objective manner.

As an example, let's begin with the design of an expert system for diagnosing problems in IBM PC compatible computers. For this computer diagnostic system, our domain is the problems that someone with limited technical skills and few tools could solve using an IBM PC compatible computer. This definition provides a search space that could be addressed on a small computer by a Turbo Prolog program using backward chaining, with limited forward chaining, and depth-first searching.

> **Goal:** By asking questions about the computer's symptoms, identify computer repair strategies that could be addressed by a user with limited technical expertise.

Some goals are not adaptable to expert system programming. The basic rules for when to use and when not to use an expert system were covered in the first chapter. In summary:

1. The problem solution should involve formal reasoning.

2. An exact procedure for solving the problem is not necessary, but there should be some heuristics available.

3. You are building a model of a human expert's reasoning process. There should be at least one human expert available.

4. It should be possible to objectively define the goal and domain, and the domain should be small enough to be manageable on the computer system that will be used.

Defining the Domain

After the goal is defined, the next step for the knowledge engineer is to define the domain of the knowledge representation. A *domain* is a definable area or extent of knowledge about a particular subject area. The domain needs to be defined objectively, and it should be small enough to be manageable on the computer that will be used.

A medical diagnostic system would encompass a large domain, probably too large and difficult to manage on even a mainframe or minicomputer. A nutritional diagnostic system might be a much smaller domain, with a rule base limited to symptoms related to nutritional problems. A diagnostic system to deal with allergies would be even a smaller domain, and probably manageable by a personal computer.

When you start to design any expert system, it is generally best to start with a small domain and gradually extend it as the value of the system with the small domain is proven. Start with a few rules to support a specifically defined domain, then expand the rules to support a larger domain.

> **Domain:** The domain will be limited to problems that can be solved with simple tools that are usually found at home or at a business. The domain should include peripherals that are used in most systems: floppy disk, hard disk, and printer.

If you want to design your own expert system, it is best to start with a domain in which you are the expert. You will feel more comfortable with each level of abstraction and can model your own thinking process. This does not have to be a large domain or represent a high level of expertise. The main purpose is to see how a computer system can model a formal thinking process.

Exercises

1. Assume you are working with a doctor of international renown in designing an expert system for nutritional analysis. The system should

be able to define nutritional deficiencies from facts ascertained during a consultation. You want to build a small prototype that will run on a personal computer, just enough to excite the doctor and get his interest in funding further development. He gives you an hour of his time. What questions would you ask him in this hour that would help in the prototype design?

2. What problems could you define in this domain representation?

3. How would you reduce the domain and search space for the prototype?

4. What subgoals can you identify?

chapter 17

Representing the Knowledge

☐ After the goal and domain have been defined, you can begin defining the model for your knowledge representation and building your system.

Deep Versus Shallow Knowledge

Now let's suppose that, as a knowledge engineer, you begin your research on building the expert system by observing a technician repair several hundred computers. With time, you see relationships between causes and effects. You observe computers coming into the shop with a variety of problems, and the technician seems to respond in specific ways to specific problems.

If the computer does not operate at all, the technician begins by opening the cabinet and checking the power supply. If the disk drive is not reading correctly, the technician checks the alignment. You then begin putting your rules together from these observations:

IF the computer does not function

AND nothing happens when the computer is turned on

THEN the power supply may be at fault.

You could continue in this way for many days and then build your expert system from what you observe, but the system would represent very shallow knowledge and would not be reliable. You never explored the root causes of any problem or tapped into the technician's knowledge about why different things were happening. If the technician had an electrical engineering degree and had attended a training program on computer repair, he or she would be working from a much deeper level of knowledge that should be captured in the expert system.

If you were building a medical diagnostic system, the problem would be even more acute. You could observe the doctor for many months, but a system built only on observations would be very dangerous to use.

This type of design approach never probes the deeper aspects of the problems, never explores the specific details of why the expert did what he or she did. Deep knowledge refers to basic theories, root causes, and facts in a specific domain. Shallow knowledge refers to basic heuristics and techniques of guessing that are used when deeper knowledge is not available.

The human mind does not distinguish so much between knowledge levels (deep or shallow) in solving a problem. A human expert does not worry about how the problem is solved, but just concentrates on solving it. In moving toward a goal, the expert may work at a shallow knowledge level one moment and at a deep knowledge level the next.

In designing an expert system, however, the distinction between deep and shallow knowledge is much more objective. The knowledge engineer has to make specific decisions as to whether deep or shallow knowledge is being used at any given time in defining the domain, goals, subgoals, rules, objects, and attributes.

Identifying the Boundaries in the Domain

The identification of boundaries in the domain defines the search space as well as where deep and shallow knowledge will be used.

1. What tools can we assume the user has at his or her disposal?
2. How much knowledge can we assume the user has and what type is needed?
3. What peripherals will be used?
4. To what detail level will the diagnosis pursue (system, board, component)?

These questions need to be defined and answered specifically and objectively before starting.

> **Object Boundaries:** The only tools assumed are screwdrivers and, perhaps, a voltmeter. The user needs a knowledge of DOS, but no technical knowledge. The only peripheral assumed in addition to the monitor is the printer. Diagnosis will be pursued to the board level, occasionally to the component level.

At this time, you are not really specifying the final objects and attributes to use; you are defining the space in which these can be defined. During this time you will probably want to define some of the objects and attributes, experimenting with a few rules to gain some insights on the problems you will encounter.

Identifying Problems in the Domain

The knowledge engineer should also identify and address key problems in the domain.

1. Computer problems can be intermittent, varying with time, temperature, or the environment. A user may see a problem once every six months, making it difficult to identify and correct.

2. Some important knowledge about the problem may be unavailable or difficult to obtain with the limited resources. For example, a technician can easily measure the power supply voltage on a disk drive board and determine if the power supply or power supply cabling is defective. The procedure is simple, but difficult to capture in a simple expert system.

3. Graphics will be needed for some fault identification. A good memory diagnostic program, for example, can draw a picture on the computer screen of the location of a defective memory chip. Such graphics are difficult to capture in a simple expert system.

4. There is wide variation between the so-called IBM PC compatibles. A problem that is evident in one compatible may not exist in another.

5. The relationship of some facts may not be clearly understood by the user. A resident program improperly installed can cause the computer to give disk write errors when trying to format a disk with the standard DOS format program. How would this information be captured?

Reducing the Search Space

One basic design strategy is to try to reduce the size of the search space as quickly as possible. If you are using backward chaining, you need to design the dialog to eliminate nonrelevant goal states as quickly as possible. The first question should eliminate at least half of the goal states. By starting with a multichoice question, you may be able to eliminate a larger percentage of the goal states.

If you are using forward chaining, you should try to identify and eliminate nonrelevant facts. This will reduce the number of rules that can fire, minimizing the search space.

You can alter the basic topology of the search space by the design

153

of the questions. Because Prolog uses backward chaining, you should try to keep the number of final goal states small in comparison with the starting facts for maximum efficiency. This may mean choosing between redefining the domain or deciding to live with less efficiency.

Identifying Subgoals

The human expert begins to solve a complex goal by trying to break the goal down to manageable subgoals. If the computer does not work, the technician first tries to determine if it is a startup problem, a run problem, or a printer problem. If it is a startup problem, the technician then tries to decide whether the initial diagnostics failed or if the boot failed.

Questions to diagnose problems at the subgoal level are defined symptomatically, not systematically. In the automotive diagnostic system, for example, the subgoals may try to define the system at fault (for example, fuel, electrical, or cooling), but the questions to the user are symptomatic questions that determine the operation of the underlying system. For example:

```
Are the headlights dead or dim when you try to turn them
     on?
```

This is a specific question about a symptom. It determines the viability of the electrical system, but it is a *symptomatic* question that relates to an observable fact. The node in the problem space (which is a subgoal) represents a symptom (headlights dead or dim) and a cause (electrical system defective). The initial nodes (subgoals) represent general causes, and as you progress the causes become more detailed. The final goal state represents a very specific cause.

The subgoals define the hierarchy and modularization of the system, and affect the overall efficiency. They imply a structuring of the domain, which in itself represents knowledge. For this reason, you will need the human expert's help in defining these subgoals.

General Guidelines

In building an expert system, you should always start with a small domain, building a small expert system or prototype and "tuning" it until it works as well as possible. The design procedure includes a lot of trial and error as you work with different subgoals and problem space designs. Eventually, a type of order may begin to emerge. The system will work, however, even if there is little formal structure or order.

Define the objects, attributes, and values and begin writing your rules. Define the questions as they relate to symptoms at each subgoal. The next chapter will guide you through this process in detail.

Before looking at the details, let's summarize the steps to this point.

1. Define the goal objectively. Be sure it is suitable for an expert system.

2. Define the domain objectively. Be sure it is a realistic domain for the resources available.

3. Become as familiar as possible with the domain.

4. Find an expert who is familiar with the domain and who will make the commitment to work with you.

5. Define the objects and attributes.

6. Identify subgoals, defining these symptomatically and systematically.

7. Identify key problem areas.

8. Be sure the shape of the search space is realistic.

9. With the expert, work through several example problems. Define the process in detail.

10. Select the tools you will use (for example, software and hardware). Do not be afraid to try several tools, comparing their values.

11. Define some rules and build a small prototype model of a small part of the domain. Test it thoroughly. Let the expert use it and exhaustively compare the prototype's operation relative to its small domain. Work with a design goal of building a limited but accurate model.

12. Use a cyclic method of adding knowledge. Add more rules, test, modify, then add again.

13. Identify any tools that can help in the design process. Purchase as necessary.

14. Document your design.

As a knowledge engineer, avoid trying to get the expert to define your IF-THEN rules. Do not give the human expert examples and then ask him or her how they would be solved. This leads to shallow knowledge. A better alternative is to build the best prototype model you can with what you know, then ask the expert to explain its weaknesses and strengths.

Exercises

1. Make a list, as you see it, of the problems in designing a diagnostic expert system for personal computers.

2. How would you evaluate the number of rules and final goal states that would be a part of the computer diagnostic system?

3. Give an example of shallow and deep knowledge rules as applied to a computer diagnostic system.

chapter $\boxed{18}$

Knowledge Acquisition

☐ Now that you have learned some general aspects of expert system design, let's construct a system. We will continue with the computer diagnostic system, defining the subgoals, objects, attributes, and rules.

The Paradigm

When an expert system is functioning, it interacts with the user with some type of problem-solving scenario, which is called the *consultation paradigm*. All expert systems of a certain type use the same general type of paradigm. For example, all diagnostic systems use a diagnostic/prescriptive paradigm. In this paradigm, the user is asked to identify symptoms or observable characteristics of a problem so that the expert system can determine which of several solutions is most appropriate. This is the most general type of paradigm for expert systems, and is the type that will be used for the computer diagnostic system.

In a production system using the diagnostic/prescriptive consultation paradigm, the highest level rules are of the form:

```
diagnosed(Z) :-
  symptom(A),
  symptom(B),
```

```
symptom(C),...
cause(X).
```

The presence of each symptom is identified using the *symptom(Y)* predicate with questions that are answered by the user. The *cause* predicate is the final output predicate.

The Strategy

In our diagnostic/prescriptive paradigm, the basic strategy for reaching a goal is to ask a specific set of questions in a consultation session with the user. The answers to the questions are used to build facts, which are stored in a Prolog dynamic database. The facts, in turn, are used to trigger and fire rules that express the relationships between the various known facts and between the facts and new conclusions. As rules fire, the conclusions are added to other existing facts and conclusions in working memory (the dynamic database). Eventually, the system either reaches one of the specified conclusions (goals) or admits that it cannot reach a conclusion based on the information available.

The most important aspect in system design is the theory of knowledge representation used—that is, the selection of objects and attributes used to represent the domain. The type and order of the rules, which depends upon the objects and attributes used, determines the eventual effectiveness of the system.

For example, if we are designing a computer diagnostic system, there is no need for the system to ask questions about the disk drive if the system display does not work. In a medical diagnostic system, there is no need to ask questions about a headache if the patient is trying to communicate that he or she has an upset stomach and there is no disease in the database that can connect a headache to an upset stomach. The selection and order of the dialog questions (which, in turn, are driven by the rules in the system) are very important in preventing useless questions and the exploration of blind alleys. The rules, in turn, are built around object-attribute-value triplets (or attribute-value pairs) that are defined by the knowledge engineer.

The solution to this problem, as we shall see, is the identification of the proper subgoals. In solving a real problem, the expert uses this same strategy. A medical doctor begins, for example, by listening to the initial complaint and then trying to decide which subsystem is at fault. It may be the pulmonary, digestive, nervous, or perhaps the circulatory system. The doctor first tries to break the primary goal down to a smaller objective: the identification of the subsystem at fault. From this, the doctor continues to further subsubgoals. It is the same as designing rules for our expert system. After the primary goal is defined, subgoals and even subsubgoals must be defined. An example is presented in this chapter.

Another aspect of the basic strategy is that the dialog process is symptomatic. The questions will be about symptoms: observations that the user can make. The user explores *effects* (symptoms) in an attempt to identify the *causes*. The consultation moves from the general (effects, symptoms, causes) to the specific (effects, symptoms, causes). Each node in the search space is both an effect and a cause. The eventual goal is to identify a cause.

Getting the Facts

After you have identified your goals, you can begin to identify facts that can help you prove each goal. In each case, you need to supply enough knowledge so that each hypothesis can be proved or disproved positively. At the same time, you should avoid including additional information that can lead to confusion or wrong conclusions. In each case, the goal is defined as a hypothesis, and is the cause. The supporting facts are defined as symptoms, and can be observed and verified by the user.

Table 18.1 shows a partial listing of the facts for our computer repair example. In most cases, you would want to create this list with a word processor, editing the listing until it meets the desired objective.

Table 18.1
Listing the Facts

Hypotheses	Symptoms
The floppy disk drive has no power.	System will not boot from the floppy disk. The floppy disk drive light does not come on. There is no noise or sound from the drive.
The floppy disk is physically defective.	If the disk contains DOS, it will not boot. The drive light comes on during boot attempt. The disk is noisy in the drive. The disk has read or write problems. It is difficult to insert or remove the disk. During boot, a 608 code is generated. A track/sector error message is displayed. In a two-drive system, the disk does not work in either drive.
The write-protect hole on the disk is covered.	You can read from the disk, but cannot write to it. You get the following message: "Write protect error reading drive X. Abort, Retry, Ignore?" The drive light comes on. The FORMAT program will not format the disk.

159

Table 18.1 (cont.)

Hypotheses	Symptoms
The floppy disk drive is out of alignment.	The disk has read or write problems. A track/sector error message is displayed. You cannot boot from the disk. The drive light comes on.
A resident program is interfering with disk reading and writing.	The disk has read or write problems. The FORMAT program will not format the disk. The drive light comes on.
A broken or defective fan belt in the drive.	You cannot boot from the drive. The drive light comes on, but the disk will not read or write. The following message is displayed: "Not ready reading drive X. Abort, Retry, Ignore?" The FORMAT program will not format the disk.
A dirty head in the disk drive.	The disk has read or write problems. A track/sector error message is displayed. You cannot boot from the disk. If you have a two-drive system, the disk works fine in the other drive.
The disk is inserted incorrectly.	You cannot boot from the disk. The drive light comes on, but the disk will not read or write. The following message is displayed: Not ready reading drive X. Abort, Retry, Ignore?" The disk label is not facing up or the edge of the disk with the read hole is not inserted first. You cannot boot from the disk. The drive light comes on. Read and write problems. The FORMAT program will not format the disk.
The drive door is not closed.	You cannot boot from the disk. The drive light comes on, but the disk will not read or write. The following message is displayed: "Not ready reading drive X. Abort, Retry, Ignore?" The disk drive door is open. The drive light comes on. Read and write problems. The FORMAT program will not format the disk.

Looking at table 18.1, we can make several observations.

1. Notice that all of the facts (symptoms) for each hypothesis are listed at a single place and not spread out, as they will be eventually in

the rule base. It is easy to see the relationship of the hypotheses and facts. This allows you to easily identify facts that are missing and facts that can confuse the goal.

2. In some cases there is an either-or situation. One set of facts or the other may be related to a hypothesis.

3. The list should reveal certain common symptoms between various hypotheses. These will be used later to define subgoals and subsubgoals. Even at this early stage, however, you should be trying to identify common symptoms.

4. This list is valuable for testing your system later. When the system is finished, you should be able to enter each list of symptoms and get the specified conclusion.

5. If you need to add rules later or edit the existing rule base, this list is valuable documentation of the design.

Charting the Facts

The next stage is to put the facts in the form of a chart. The column headings are the hypotheses and the row headings are the symptoms. If you have a spreadsheet program, you can use it to create this chart. An example of a chart for part of our computer diagnostic system is shown in table 18.2.

Table 18.2
Charting the Facts

Symptoms	Hypotheses								
	Drive has no power	Disk defective	Write-protect hole covered	Drive out of alignment	Resident program problem	Broken belt	Dirty head	Disk inserted incorrectly	Disk door not closed
Does not boot	XXXXX	XXXXX		XXXXX		XXXXX	XXXXX	XXXXX	XXXXX
Drive light does not come on	XXXXX								
No sound from drive	XXXXX								
Drive light comes on		XXXXX	XXXXX	XXXXX	XXXXX	XXXXX	XXXXX	XXXXX	XXXXX
Drive is noisy		XXXXX				XXXXX			
Read problems		XXXXX		XXXXX	XXXXX	XXXXX	XXXXX	XXXXX	XXXXX
Write problems		XXXXX	XXXXX	XXXXX	XXXXX	XXXXX	XXXXX	XXXXX	XXXXX
Difficult to insert disk		XXXXX							
During initial diagnostics, a 608 code		XXXXX							
Track/sector error message		XXXXX		XXXXX			XXXXX		

Table 18.2 (cont.)

Symptoms	Drive has no power	Disk de-fective	Write-protect hole covered	Drive out of align-ment	Resident program problem	Broken belt	Dirty head	Disk in-serted incor-rectly	Disk door not closed
Disk does not work in any drive		XXXXX							
Write protect message			XXXXX						
FORMAT program does not format the disk			XXXXX		XXXXX	XXXXX	XXXXX	XXXXX	XXXXX
Not ready reading message						XXXXX		XXXXX	XXXXX
Disk works in other drive				XXXXX			XXXXX		
Disk label not facing up								XXXXX	
Drive door open									XXXXX

The final chart may be several pages long. If some conclusions have symptoms not related to other conclusions, you may want to chart these separately. The primary purpose of the chart is to help you see relatedness and to help identify subgoals and subsubgoals.

Identifying Common Factors

After you have made the chart, you should try to rechart the list with a smaller group of symptoms that represent generalizations of previous symptoms. Your original chart may have hundreds of facts. Some of these facts should have some common denominator. By identifying this common fact, you can construct a path to more detailed questions. Again, you should use the hypotheses as column headings and the symptoms as row headings (see table 18.3).

Table 18.3
Summary Chart

Symptoms	Drive has no power	Disk de-fective	Write-protect hole covered	Drive out of align-ment	Resident program problem	Broken belt	Dirty head	Disk in-serted incor-rectly	Disk door not closed
Initial diagnostics/startup problems	XXXXX	XXXXX		XXXXX		XXXXX	XXXXX	XXXXX	XXXXX
RUN problems	XXXXX	XXXXX	XXXXX	XXXXX	XXXXX	XXXXX	XXXXX	XXXXX	XXXXX

As an example, in a medical diagnostic system you could ask the general question: "Does the patient have a cough?" If the answer was yes, you could then pursue more detailed questions about the type of cough (moderate, harsh, hacking). In a computer diagnostic system, you could ask the general question: "Is the display working correctly?" If the answer was no, you could then pursue more detailed questioning about the type of problem with the display. This is part of your subgoal identification process.

This structuring or modularization is not an easy process with many systems, and in some systems it is only partially applicable. Spend some time trying to do as much factoring as possible, but do not worry if some facts cannot be factored. Whatever you can do will simplify the design process later and also make it easier for the user to use the system.

The Structured Approach

Your next strategy is the creation of the decision tree that will form the basic structure of the program. The strategy is to try to start by asking a question that will eliminate at least 50 percent of the search space. Notice that if you start with a multichoice question, you can usually eliminate 75 percent or more of the search space. The questions should go from the general to the specific. Perhaps the easiest way to do this properly is to create a decision tree such as the one in figure 18.1. Each node in this tree represents a question (symptom) in the expert system. The links represent answers to questions. A yes or no question will have two branches; a multichoice question can have many. You may also have questions in which the user can enter the attribute value, such as:

How many beeps do you hear when the system is turned on?

As with a multichoice question, this would be represented by a node with several branches.

The eventual diagram may look more like a network than an inverted tree. There may be several paths to the same conclusion or to the same subgoal or subsubgoal. This is normal and Prolog can support such constructs easily.

The actual design process from the facts to the decision tree is quite cyclic. You may get to this point and see that no visible decision tree emerges and find yourself at a dead end with plenty of facts and conclusions but no structure. Sometimes the expert can help you find order, but often the structure eludes even the expert. This is, in fact, one of the best features of the expert system—even if you cannot define any structure, the system will still work. The structure or decision tree, in essence, is a heuristic that you are applying to the system to simplify the consultation process. There is no real guarantee that it will be the best heuristic, and the system will still work if no structure is used. The

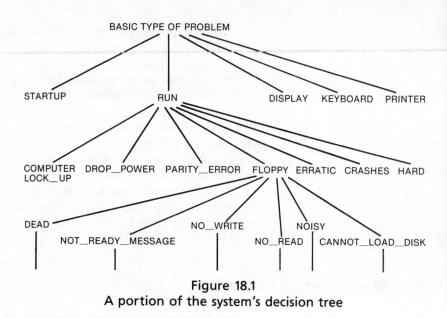

Figure 18.1
A portion of the system's decision tree

knowledge engineer, working with the expert, tries to define the best heuristic (decision tree or structure) possible.

Writing the Rules

After you have completed the decision tree, you are ready to begin writing the rules and defining the questions. Normally you will work from the left to the right of your decision tree, converting the nodes and links to Prolog rules—thus creating the rules that lead to the eventual conclusion.

Each node in the search space represents both a cause and an effect. The question is about the symptom; the symptom at the node represents the effect. The answer determines the cause; the cause controls the branching.

Look again at the automotive diagnostic system. At one node we need to determine if voltage is getting to the starter motor and relay (in other words, if the battery voltage is correct and whether or not the battery connections are good). This is a cause. The effect (symptom) is that the headlights are dim or do not work at all when turned on. The question is asked in terms of the effect or symptom. You can store either the effect or the cause in the database as an A-V pair:

```
headlights,dim
```

or an O-A-V triplet:

```
electrical_power,false
```

In either case, you identify the node in the search space to the database, and indicate that the search successfully got to that node or that the node failed.

At some level in the decision tree, the final goal is hypothesized. We suspect the cause, but have not identified it positively. At this point, you will need to ask specific and detailed questions to identify the conclusion with certainty. Always be sure you use enough facts to prove the final conclusion true.

> **Note:** In some types of systems, it is impossible to prove a conclusion with complete certainty. In this case, you will need to use special techniques that are discussed in chapter 19.

Testing

After the system is developed, it must be tested. The charts and tables used to design the system are the best launching point for the test, but you will probably find that your system has evolved somewhat from these and the rules do not match exactly. At this point, you must do a little reverse engineering, rewriting the initial charts and facts and retesting based on the new charts. This is a cyclic process; you rewrite the rules, update the charts, rewrite the rules, and then update the charts again.

The Explanatory Interface

A good expert system should permit the user to ask why in response to questions. For example, the computer might ask:

```
If you have a two-drive system, does the disk work in
     the other drive?
```

The user may answer with a question mark, to which the system replies:

```
If you have a second drive, you can isolate the problem
     between the disk and the drive. If the problem
     moves to the other drive with the same disk,
     the problem is the software or the disk. If the
     problem does not move, the problem is in the
     hardware: the drive, controller, cable, or power
     supply.
```

Dealing with Unknowns

There may be situations in which the user does not know the answer to a question. The answer may require equipment not available to the user, such as:

What is the power supply voltage at the disk drive?

This assumes the user has a voltmeter, which may not be true. In other cases, the user may simply not understand the question:

What is the date on your computer system ROM?

In either case, the user should be able to answer in a way that acknowledges that the answer is unknown, and the system should be able to backtrack and find additional rules to get to the desired goal state.

Summary

As a review, the following is a summary of the design of our expert system.

1. Define the goal of the system (objective).

2. Define the domain. How realistic is the goal and domain as defined? Redefine the problem definition as necessary.

3. Define the knowledge representation model: objects, properties, relationships, and deep versus shallow representations.

4. Identify the problem areas in the representation and domain. Is the data reliable? Is it static? Are the relationships known?

5. Begin acquiring the knowledge. Build the representation.

6. Define the decision tree and build a small prototype.

7. Test the prototype.

8. Analyze and redesign.

9. Test again.

10. Expand the system, adding more rules and knowledge.

11. Test, analyze, and redesign.

Exercises

1. Design a small expert system that can be used to determine if a problem can be solved with an expert system on a personal computer. Use Turbo Prolog to design the system.

2. How would you test the system in exercise 1? Document a test procedure for a technician not acquainted with expert system design.

3. Redesign the *check* and *checkc* predicates in the computer diagnostic program (see appendix B) to enable the user to enter a question mark when he wants to know why a particular question is asked. (Note: It is not necessary to enter the whole program for this exercise. Enter a partial set of clauses and modify them for the exercise.)

chapter 19

Dealing with Uncertainty

□ In the previous chapter, the knowledge rules used for the reasoning process were expressed as a relationship of certain facts. It is not unusual, however, for some attribute values to be missing or known with a less than certain value.

For example, the expert system might ask:

```
Does the floppy disk drive motor turn?
```

The user may not know what a floppy disk motor is or the motor may turn sometimes. There may be no simple yes or no answer. How can we take this into account when designing our rules?

There is no one method for best accomplishing this objective, but this chapter will introduce you to three methods of dealing with this uncertainty: fuzzy logic, certainty factors, and probability.

Fuzzy Logic

In a simple expert system, the questions are normally designed for a binary response of either yes or no. A yes answer implies a true value (1), and a no answer implies a false value (0).

In some cases, a rule may need to express a partial truth, so the answer is not a clear yes or no. For example:

```
Is the subject a child?
```

The answer depends upon what is meant by *child*.

Fuzzy logic permits us to answer such a question and use the result to propagate the fact to other rules. The user is not bound to a simple yes or no answer.

Fuzzy logic was originally invented by Lotfi Zadeh in 1965 to extend the concepts of Boolean logic to formal reasoning. In Boolean logic, false is represented by 0 and true by 1. There are only two logic values permitted. In fuzzy logic, truth values can range from 0 to 1, and can thus be used to represent partial truths.

The basic rules for evaluating a premise using fuzzy logic are as follows:

p1 AND p2 AND p3 = MIN(p1,p2,p3)

p1 OR p2 OR p3 = MAX(p1,p2,p3)

NOT p1 = 1−p1

For example:

IF Bob drives a Pontiac (.5)

AND Sue likes Pontiacs (.8)

THEN Sue will let Bob drive her to the game Saturday.

In this example, Bob's car is really a modified (shall we say) Pontiac that is rather unique (truth value of .5). Sue is only moderately crazy about Pontiacs (truth value of .8). The resulting truth value is .5, so Bob's chances of having Sue accept his offer for a date based on what we know is 50 percent—the minimum of the two values.

Suppose we add a second rule:

IF Bob is a very interesting conversationalist (.8)

AND Sue enjoys good conversationalists (.85)

THEN Sue will let Bob drive her to the game Saturday.

This time the truth value of the conclusion is again the minimum, or .8. The two conclusions (.5 and .8) are ORed, so we get the maximum value of .5 and .8. Bob's chances of getting the date are now 80 percent.

Certainty Factors

Fuzzy logic can be used for partial truths, but sometimes information is lacking and simply not available. In a more general case, information is known but not with certainty.

For example, in a medical diagnostic system, certain symptoms may be indicative of a specific disease, but the symptoms or diagnosis may not be certain. A baby may be crying from an acute stomach pain, but the doctor may not be certain of the symptom (stomach pain) because the baby cannot communicate verbally. Even if there was a way to determine the symptom with absolute certainty, the hypothesis (colic) is not the only possible conclusion, and there is only a relative certainty as to it being the true problem.

Adding Certainty Factors to Rules

One of the major contributions of Shortliffe's work with the MYCIN expert system project was the development of what he called *certainty factors* (CFs). Certainty factors (also called *confidence factors*) are used to express the confidence of a given conclusion based on the evidence available at a given point.

As an example, let's use a rule for a fictitious medical diagnostic system. The general form of the rule would be:

```
disease(Z) :-
   symptom(A),
   cause(X).

disease(Z) :-
   symptom(B),
   cause(Y).
```

A more specific form of the rule might be:

```
disease(milk_allergy) :-
   symptom(acute_stomach_pain),
   cause(just_drank_milk).

disease(milk_allergy) :-
   symptom(diarrhea),
   cause(just_drank_milk).
```

You could continue with the rules, adding more as necessary. The observance of each symptom adds confidence in the final conclusion, but there is no way to be absolutely sure of the conclusion. The individual symptoms alone give less indication. An acute stomach pain could be caused by appendicitis or an obstruction. If enough symptoms are available, however, you can obtain a growing confidence that the conclusion is true.

> **Note:** The rules used in these examples are for illustration only. They are not endorsed by any medical doctor or organization and should not be used for diagnostic purposes.

Now let's see how we can improve this rule. We can express the confidence threshold of a particular goal in the antecedent as a value that must be exceeded for the goal to succeed. For example:

```
disease(milk_allergy) :-
  symptom(acute_stomach_pain, .2),
  cause(just_drank_milk,.8).

disease(milk_allergy) :-
  symptom(diarrhea,.4),
  cause(just_drank_milk,.8).
```

Let's imagine a doctor examining a small baby who is crying and unable to express any symptoms verbally. This first rule states that:

IF there is a 20% confidence that there is an acute stomach pain

AND there is an 80% certainty that the baby just drank milk

THEN there is a milk allergy problem.

The resulting conclusion can then be added to working memory and used to fire other rules.

The use of certainty factors in this way permits us to reason to a conclusion when certain input information is missing or unknown.

Using Certainty Factors

Calculating the confidence of a conclusion is a procedural aspect of expert systems, but it is quite different from calculating probability and other types of statistical calculations. You cannot simply multiply the values to get a resulting confidence. You also cannot add the individual confidence factors because the total is often greater than 1.

Let's look at the two rules again:

```
/* RULE 1 */
H1   disease(milk_allergy) :-
E1.1     symptom(acute_stomach_pain,.2),
E1.2     cause(just_drank_milk,.8).

/* RULE 2 */
H2   disease(milk_allergy) :-
E2.1     symptom(diarrhea,.4),
E2.2     cause(just_drank_milk,.8).
```

We can use fuzzy logic to get a certainty value of .2 for the first rule, and .4 for the second rule. If we combine these with fuzzy logic, our conclusion has a certainty of .4, or 40 percent. Adding more symptoms does not necessarily improve the certainty of the conclusion. Clearly, we need a better way of calculating the confidence in the conclusions.

Now let's try certainty factor calculations. Shortliffe defined three terms:

CF[h:e] Certainty of hypothesis *h* given *e*

MB[h:e] Measure of belief in *h* given *e*

MD[h:e] Measure of disbelief in *h* given *e*

The certainty factor is simply the difference of the other two components:

CF[h:e] = MB[h:e] − MD[h:e]

Measures of belief (MB) and measures of disbelief (MD) can range from 0 to 1. Confidence values (CF) can range from −1 to 1.

The resulting MB for our rules could be calculated as:

MB[h] = MB[h1] + MB[h2](1 − MB[h1])

The first MB is added to the total:

MB = MB[h1] = .2

Then the distance to total confidence is measured:

1 − .2 = .8

The second value (MB[h2] or .8) is then multiplied by the second value (.8):

MB = .8 × .8 = .64

This is then added to the first total:

MB = .2 + .64 = .84

Notice that if the first certainty factor increased to .3, the total MB becomes .86, a slightly higher value.

Sometimes the conclusion itself has a certain confidence based on the premises being true. This confidence factor can be expressed as a certainty factor that is used to multiply the confidence factor calculated from the premises:

IF there is abdominal soreness (.4)

AND there is an acute stomach pain (.6)

THEN there is an indication of appendicitis (.8).

This rule states that if we are 40 percent certain there is abdominal soreness and 60 percent certain there is an acute stomach pain, we can be 80 percent certain of appendicitis. (Again, this is a fictional rule to illustrate a concept.)

How this knowledge would be propagated to other rules depends upon reality. As an example, we could use confidence factors:

CF = (.4 + (.6 × (1 − .4))) × .8 = .608

We would then store the resulting attribute (indication), value (appendicitis), and certainty factor in working memory to use for testing other rules.

We could also include evidence against a conclusion or contraindications in a rule (measure of disbelief). For example, if there is abdominal soreness, this would be a contraindication for milk allergy. If the condition is contraindicative, the distance to 0 is measured (instead of the distance to 1) and then multiplied by the measure of disbelief. The value is then subtracted from the total.

From these examples you can make several observations:

1. The order of the rules does not matter.

2. The combined measure of belief is higher than that of any individual measure of belief. As more symptoms are added to the rule, we can increase our confidence in the final answer and provide additional confidence when knowledge is lacking for any particular symptom.

It should be emphasized that none of these formulas has a statistical interpretation. There is, in fact, no reason even to accept the results of the formulas except that they have been found to work in many applications. If both the MB and MD are high, this indicates a large amount of contradictory evidence. If both are low, there is a lack of evidence. In general, the equations are most effective if one is high and the other low.

After the certainty of a conclusion is established, the conclusion with its certainty can become part of the antecedent for another rule. The basic rules, as used in MYCIN, can be expressed as follows:

- Rule 1: If a premise succeeds with a definite certainty, then the value is concluded with its attached certainty. This conclusion, with its attached CF, is propagated to other rules.

- Rule 2: If the premise succeeds but has a certainty factor associated with it, then the final certainty factor is obtained by multiplying the conclusion certainty factor and the premise certainty factor.

To prevent the firing of a large number of rules with low confidence levels, the system is normally designed so that only rules that have a resulting certainty above a certain threshold (for example, .2 in MYCIN) are considered for firing. After being fired, the conclusion (attribute, value, and certainty factor) is added to the database.

Probability

Although certainty factors and fuzzy logic are the predominate theories used in expert systems, there are occasions when probabilities are an important part of the reasoning process. Probability computations, more generally called Bayesianism, are based on Baye's Theorem:

$$LR[H:E] = p[E:H]/p[E:H']$$

which formally states that the likelihood of a hypothesis is equal to the probability of the evidence given a particular hypothesis divided by the probability of the evidence given the falsity of that hypothesis. If you are planning an expert system to predict football games, you would probably be more interested in probabilities than certainty factors.

Reality

In designing good expert systems, you are building a model of reality. There is no "best method," or any method, that has been proven mathematically correct. The approach for a particular rule or system is determined by what the system is modeling and by reality. You should make your decision about what equations to use by what the system is supposed to do. The expert system is a model of reality, and the model is only meaningful in the sense that you have found a good algorithm to use in modeling a particular part of the formal reasoning process. If you can find equations and procedures that work better than those in this book, you should use them.

With any system, you must define calculation methods for the following situations. These calculation methods are based on how your model should resolve the corresponding logic.

- Conjunction (AND). A conjunction is the combination of two conditions such that the goal is satisfied only if both of the conditions are satisfied. An example is the joining of two goals with an AND as the antecedent of a rule. If each goal has a certainty factor, what is the certainty factor of the combined antecedent?
- Disjunction (OR). A disjunction results if either of two goals must be satisfied for the conclusion to be satisfied. Disjunctions are created in expert systems by using two rules with the same conclusion. If each rule has a certainty factor, what is the resulting certainty factor?
- Conclusion Resolution. The conclusion, as well as the premise, may have a certainty factor. How is the resulting certainty factor calculated?
- Sign. Certainty factors can be positive or negative. How are negative values processed?

Refer to table 19.1 for an overview of the three methods of calculating certainty factors explained in this chapter.

Table 19.1
Methods of Certainty Factor Calculation

Method	Conjunction	Disjunction	CF Rule for Conclusion
Fuzzy logic	Minimum	Maximum	CF of conclusion
Probability	A × B	A + (1 − A) × B	CF antecedent × CF conclusion
Certainty	*	*	CF antecedent × CF conclusion

*See text.

Using Rules with Uncertainty

In some systems, you can deal with uncertainty by adding rules and heuristics that specifically address the uncertainty. For example, suppose the following question is asked in a medical diagnostic system that is trying to diagnose an allergy to an inhalant:

`Does the patient have eczema?`

Suppose the user does not know what eczema is. With normal reasoning, the response would be "unknown" and the reasoning would continue, trying to find a path to the conclusion based on other symptoms. You could, however, sense the "unknown" answer and use additional rules to ask about eczema symptoms. These answers, in turn, determine whether the patient has eczema and the truth of the eczema question.

Exercise

Write a Prolog program that uses a *check* predicate to input the certainty of a truth (instead of yes or no). Write a new *diagnosed* predicate in which the conclusion can be specified with a certainty as:

```
diagnosed(starter_motor,.8).
```

Design the output routine to output the resulting goal state with its certainty.

Conclusion

Today, it is possible for a person with a microcomputer, an inexpensive Turbo Prolog program, and a little technical expertise to begin developing expert systems that can do useful work.

Even with what we know, however, the techniques of expert system design are still emerging. There is no standard Prolog, and all of the expert system languages have serious shortcomings. There is no standard vocabulary or even a general theory of knowledge representation that would apply to all domains. Knowledge engineering remains as one of the fastest growing challenges in computer science.

appendix A

Turbo Prolog Versus Other Prologs

☐ Borland's Turbo Prolog has both strengths and weaknesses in comparison with other Prolog compilers on the market. Other Prolog versions are built from the Clocksin and Mellish (C & M) model. If you have programming experience, you will probably be more comfortable with Turbo Prolog. But a veteran AI "hacker" might find Turbo Prolog's divergence from the C & M versions difficult to accept.

C & M Prolog is not a typed language. As a result, compiling is slower than with Turbo Prolog, error checking abilities are limited, and the resulting code runs slower. Turbo Prolog, as a result of typing, is compiled and executed faster and provides more resource control for the developer.

Because predicate arguments are not declared in C & M Prolog, predicates can accept multiple types. In Turbo Prolog, predicates can only accept multiple types by declaring them with multiple declarations in the predicates section. As a result, Turbo Prolog has a few symbolic programming constraints. For example, you cannot declare a domain that allows arbitrary functor names, and a domain cannot define alternatives that take different argument types for the same functor.

Turbo Prolog provides an extensive library of built-in predicates that are unavailable or cost extra with other compilers. Predicates are included for windowing, PC graphics modes, several EGA modes, plotting points, drawing lines, and turtle graphics. File predicates are included for sequential and random access. Like C & M versions, you can redirect keyboard and screen I/O to other devices. With Turbo Prolog, you can also access Borland's editor from within an executing program to edit input. There are also plenty of low-level predicates for bit manipulation, DOS system access, and both peeking and poking.

Turbo Prolog's static database is limited by the amount of computer memory available. This ensures a fast running system, but limits its applicability such that it can only be used with small domains. With a little programming expertise, Turbo Prolog's dynamic databases can be stored on disk. For larger rule bases, you will probably find that other Prologs are better. For example, Arity's Prolog supports virtual memory; that is, the disk is used as an extension of memory, permitting the support of large rule bases up to gigabyte size. Do not expect a virtual memory system to function as fast as a true memory-resident system, but with a RAMdisk and Arity's Prolog you can gain fairly fast access to a personal computer expert system that can be much larger than one Turbo Prolog could support.

As an overview, Turbo Prolog is a remarkable development product for anyone beginning with expert system design. There is a lot of Prolog included for a very low cost. It is a very fast language, and is easily learned by programmers familiar with traditional programming languages.

appendix B

Diagnostic Expert System Listing

□ The author makes no warranty to the effectiveness or accuracy of this listing. A current source code copy of the latest release can be ordered in electronic form for $19.95 postpaid from: PC EXPERT SYSTEM, Oregon Professional Microsystems, 4110 N.E. Alameda, Portland, OR 97212. The source code is available in IBM PC compatible disk format only. The listing (and this book) is copyrighted, and should not be copied in any form without the written permission of the copyright owner.

The rules are based, in part, on material in the following books:

Brenner, Robert C. *IBM PC Troubleshooting and Repair Guide.* Indianapolis: Howard W. Sams, 1985.

Hilsman, Hoyt. *Micro Doctor: Care, Troubleshooting, and Simple Repair for Your IBM PC.* Boston: Little, Brown and Company, 1986.

To compile the listing with Turbo Prolog, you will need a minimum of 640K memory. This system is about the maximum size you can use for an expert system in Turbo Prolog on an IBM XT. Spaces at the beginning of each line should be converted to tabs to reduce storage space.

Listing B.1
Computer diagnostic expert system for IBM PC compatible computers

```
/*      COMPUTER DIAGNOSTIC EXPERT SYSTEM
          for IBM PC Compatible Computers
*/

code=3072
database
dbase(symbol,char)


predicates
run
title
diagnosed(symbol)
diag(symbol)
checkc(symbol,char)
check(symbol)
clear_facts
response(char)
repeat
run_once
cause(symbol)


goal
run.


clauses

run :-
  run_once,
  clear_facts,
  write("\nWould you like another consultation? "),
  readchar(Reply),
  write(Reply),nl,
  Reply='y',
  run.

run_once :-
  title,nl,diagnosed(_),!,clear_facts.

run_once :-
  write("\nUnable to determine what"),nl,
  write("your problem is. \n"),clear_facts.
```

Listing B.1 (cont.)

```
title :-
  clearwindow,
  write("IBM PC/XT DIAGNOSTIC EXPERT SYSTEM"),nl,nl.

repeat.
repeat :- repeat.

clear_facts:-
  retract(dbase(_,_)),fail.

clear_facts :- nl.

diagnosed(ac_power):-
  checkc(system,'1'),
  checkc(startup,'2'),
  not(check(power)),
  cause(ac_power).

diagnosed(switch):-
  checkc(system,'1'),
  checkc(startup,'2'),
  check(power),
  cause(switch).

diagnosed(no_power) :-
  checkc(system,'1'),
  checkc(startup,'3'),
  cause(no_power).

diagnosed(power_supply) :-
  checkc(system,'1'),
  checkc(startup,'1'),
  checkc(beep,'1'),
  cause(power_supply).

diagnosed(power_supply) :-
  checkc(system,'1'),
  checkc(startup,'1'),
  checkc(beep,'3'),
  cause(power_supply).

diagnosed(system_board) :-
  checkc(system,'1'),
  checkc(startup,'1'),
  checkc(beep,'4'),
  cause(system_board).
```

```
diagnosed(display) :-
  checkc(system,'1'),
  checkc(startup,'1'),
  checkc(beep,'5'),
  cause(display).


diagnosed(display) :-
  checkc(system,'1'),
  checkc(startup,'1'),
  checkc(beep,'6'),
  cause(display).


diagnosed(power_supply) :-
  checkc(system,'1'),
  checkc(startup,'1'),
  checkc(beep,'7'),
  cause(power_supply).


diagnosed(disk_drive) :-
  checkc(system,'1'),
  checkc(startup,'1'),
  checkc(beep,'8'),
  cause(disk_drive).


diagnosed(dummy) :-
  checkc(system,'1'),
  checkc(startup,'1'),
  checkc(beep,'2'),
  check(one_beep),
  diag(floppy_disk_boot).


diagnosed(memory) :-
  checkc(system,'1'),
  checkc(startup,'1'),
  not(check(memory)),
  cause(memory).


diagnosed(system_board) :-
  checkc(system,'1'),
  checkc(startup,'1'),
  check(memory),
  checkc(errorcode,'b'),
  cause(system_board2).
```

```
diagnosed(memory) :-
  checkc(system,'1'),
  checkc(startup,'1'),
  check(memory),
  checkc(errorcode,'c'),
  cause(memory).

diagnosed(keyboard) :-
  checkc(system,'1'),
  checkc(startup,'1'),
  check(memory),
  checkc(errorcode,'d'),
  cause(keyboard).

diagnosed(floppy) :-
  checkc(system,'1'),
  checkc(startup,'1'),
  check(memory),
  checkc(errorcode,'e'),
  cause(disk_drive).

diagnosed(mono_monitor) :-
  checkc(system,'1'),
  checkc(startup,'1'),
  check(memory),
  checkc(errorcode,'f'),
  cause(mono_monitor).

diagnosed(color_monitor) :-
  checkc(system,'1'),
  checkc(startup,'1'),
  check(memory),
  checkc(errorcode,'g'),
  cause(color_monitor).

diagnosed(printer) :-
  checkc(system,'1'),
  checkc(startup,'1'),
  check(memory),
  checkc(errorcode,'h'),
  cause(printer).

diagnosed(game_adapter) :-
  checkc(system,'1'),
  checkc(startup,'1'),
  check(memory),
  checkc(errorcode,'i'),
  cause(game_adapter).
```

Listing B.1 (cont.)

```
diagnosed(printer) :-
  checkc(system,'1'),
  checkc(startup,'1'),
  check(memory),
  checkc(errorcode,'j'),
  cause(power_supply).


diagnosed(hard_disk) :-
  checkc(system,'1'),
  checkc(startup,'1'),
  check(memory),
  checkc(errorcode,'k'),
  cause(hard_disk).


diagnosed(expansion_unit) :-
  checkc(system,'1'),
  checkc(startup,'1'),
  check(memory),
  checkc(errorcode,'l'),
  cause(expansion_unit).


diagnosed(power_supply) :-
  checkc(system,'1'),
  checkc(startup,'1'),
  check(memory),
  checkc(errorcode,'m'),
  cause(power_supply).


diagnosed(hard_disk) :-
  checkc(system,'1'),
  checkc(startup,'4'),
  check(hard_disk),
  check(floppy_disk_boot),
  check(dos),
  not(check(hard)),
  cause(hard_disk).


diagnosed(dos) :-
  checkc(system,'1'),
  checkc(startup,'4'),
  check(hard_disk),
  check(floppy_disk_boot),
  not(check(dos)),
  cause(dos).
```

Listing B.1 (cont.)

```
diagnosed(hard_disk) :-
  checkc(system,'1'),
  checkc(startup,'4'),
  check(hard_disk),
  check(floppy_disk_boot),
  check(dos),
  check(hard),
  not(check(boot_read_hard)),
  cause(boot_read_hard).


diagnosed(hard_disk) :-
  checkc(system,'1'),
  checkc(startup,'4'),
  check(hard_disk),
  check(floppy_disk_boot),
  check(dos),
  check(hard),
  check(boot_read_hard),
  check(boot_write_hard),
  cause(bad_dos).


diagnosed(hard_disk) :-
  checkc(system,'1'),
  checkc(startup,'4'),
  check(hard_disk),
  check(floppy_disk_boot),
  check(dos),
  check(hard),
  check(boot_read_hard),
  not(check(boot_write_hard)),
  check(autoexec),
  cause(autoexec).


diagnosed(hard_disk) :-
  checkc(system,'1'),
  checkc(startup,'4'),
  check(hard_disk),
  check(floppy_disk_boot),
  check(dos),
  check(hard),
  check(boot_read_hard),
  not(check(boot_write_hard)),
  not(check(autoexec)),
  check(config),
  cause(config).
```

```
diagnosed(hard_disk) :-
  checkc(system,'1'),
  checkc(startup,'4'),
  check(hard_disk),
  check(floppy_disk_boot),
  check(dos),
  check(hard),
  check(boot_read_hard),
  not(check(boot_write_hard)),
  not(check(autoexec)),
  not(check(config)),
  cause(unknown).

diagnosed(floppy_disk) :-
  checkc(system,'1'),
  checkc(startup,'4'),
  not(check(hard_disk)),
  diag(floppy_disk_boot).

diagnosed(floppy_disk) :-
  checkc(system,'1'),
  checkc(startup,'4'),
  check(hard_disk),
  not(check(floppy_disk_boot)),
  diag(floppy_disk_boot).

diagnosed(environment) :-
  checkc(system,'2'),
  not(check(environment)),
  cause(environment).

diagnosed(busy) :-
  checkc(system,'2'),
  checkc(run,'1'),
  check(environment),
  check(busy),
  cause(busy).

diagnosed(unplugged) :-
  checkc(system,'2'),
  checkc(run,'1'),
  check(environment),
  not(check(busy)),
  not(check(unplugged)),
  cause(unplugged).
```

Listing B.1 (cont.)

```
diagnosed(software) :-
  checkc(system,'2'),
  checkc(run,'1'),
  check(environment),
  not(check(busy)),
  check(unplugged),
  not(check(reboot)),
  cause(hardware).

diagnosed(software) :-
  checkc(system,'2'),
  checkc(run,'1'),
  check(environment),
  not(check(busy)),
  check(unplugged),
  check(reboot),
  check(repeat),
  cause(software).

diagnosed(static) :-
  checkc(system,'2'),
  checkc(run,'1'),
  check(environment),
  not(check(busy)),
  check(unplugged),
  check(reboot),
  not(check(repeat)),
  cause(static).

diagnosed(drop_power) :-
  checkc(system,'2'),
  checkc(run,'2'),
  check(environment),
  cause(drop_power).

diagnosed(parity_error) :-
  checkc(system,'2'),
  checkc(run,'3'),
  check(environment),
  cause(parity_error).

diagnosed(crashes) :-
  checkc(system,'2'),
  checkc(run,'4'),
  check(environment),
  cause(crashes).
```

```
diagnosed(software) :-
  checkc(system,'2'),
  checkc(run,'5'),
  check(environment),
  check(consistent),
  cause(erratic_software).

diagnosed(hardware) :-
  checkc(system,'2'),
  checkc(run,'5'),
  check(environment),
  not(check(consistent)),
  cause(drop_power).

diagnosed(program) :-
  checkc(system,'2'),
  checkc(run,'6'),
  check(environment),
  check(run_program),
  cause(run_program_dos).

diagnosed(program) :-
  checkc(system,'2'),
  checkc(run,'6'),
  check(environment),
  not(check(run_program)),
  cause(run_program_application).

diagnosed(hard_disk) :-
  checkc(system,'2'),
  checkc(run,'7'),
  checkc(run_hard_disk,'1'),
  check(expansion),
  cause(expansion).

diagnosed(hard_disk) :-
  checkc(system,'2'),
  checkc(run,'7'),
  checkc(run_hard_disk,'1'),
  not(check(expansion)),
  cause(run_hard_disk).

diagnosed(hard_disk) :-
  checkc(system,'2'),
  checkc(run,'7'),
  checkc(run_hard_disk,'1'),
  check(expansion),
  cause(run_expansion).
```

Listing B.1 (cont.)

```prolog
diagnosed(hard_disk) :-
  checkc(system,'2'),
  checkc(run,'7'),
  checkc(run_hard_disk,'2'),
  check(run_disk_software),
  cause(run_disk_software).

diagnosed(hard_disk) :-
  checkc(system,'2'),
  checkc(run,'7'),
  checkc(run_hard_disk,'2'),
  not(check(run_disk_software)),
  not(check(run_resident)),
  cause(run_resident).

diagnosed(hard_disk) :-
  checkc(system,'2'),
  checkc(run,'7'),
  checkc(run_hard_disk,'2'),
  not(check(run_disk_software)),
  check(run_resident),
  cause(run_harddisk_write).

diagnosed(hard_disk) :-
  checkc(system,'2'),
  checkc(run,'7'),
  checkc(run_hard_disk,'3'),
  check(run_disk_software),
  cause(run_disk_software).

diagnosed(hard_disk) :-
  checkc(system,'2'),
  checkc(run,'7'),
  checkc(run_hard_disk,'3'),
  not(check(run_disk_software)),
  not(check(run_resident)),
  cause(run_resident).

diagnosed(hard_disk) :-
  checkc(system,'2'),
  checkc(run,'7'),
  checkc(run_hard_disk,'3'),
  not(check(run_disk_software)),
  check(run_resident),
  cause(run_harddisk_write).
```

```
diagnosed(hard disk) :-
  checkc(system,'2'),
  checkc(run,'7'),
  checkc(run_hard_disk,'4'),
  cause(run_harddisk_chkdsk).


diagnosed(hard_disk) :-
  checkc(system,'2'),
  checkc(run,'7'),
  checkc(run_hard_disk,'5'),
  cause(run_harddisk_noisy).


diagnosed(hard_disk) :-
  checkc(system,'2'),
  checkc(run,'7'),
  checkc(run_hard_disk,'6'),
  check(physical_move),
  cause(physical_move).


diagnosed(hard_disk) :-
  checkc(system,'2'),
  checkc(run,'7'),
  checkc(run_hard_disk,'6'),
  not(check(physical_move)),
  cause(run_hard).


diagnosed(floppy_disk) :-
  checkc(system,'2'),
  checkc(run,'8'),
  checkc(run_floppy_disk,'1'),
  cause(run_floppy_power).


diagnosed(floppy_disk) :-
  checkc(system,'2'),
  checkc(run,'8'),
  checkc(run_floppy_disk,'2'),
  cause(run_floppy_not_ready).


diagnosed(floppy_disk) :-
  checkc(system,'2'),
  checkc(run,'8'),
  checkc(run_floppy_disk,'3'),
  not(check(run_floppy_physical)),
  cause(run_floppy_physical).
```

Listing B.1 (cont.)

```prolog
diagnosed(floppy_disk) :-
  checkc(system,'2'),
  checkc(run,'8'),
  checkc(run_floppy_disk,'3'),
  check(run_floppy_physical),
  not(check(run_resident)),
  cause(run_resident).

diagnosed(floppy_disk) :-
  checkc(system,'2'),
  checkc(run,'8'),
  checkc(run_floppy_disk,'3'),
  check(run_floppy_physical),
  check(run_resident),
  check(run_twodisks),
  check(second_disk),
  cause(bad_floppy).

diagnosed(floppy_disk) :-
  checkc(system,'2'),
  checkc(run,'8'),
  checkc(run_floppy_disk,'3'),
  check(run_floppy_physical),
  check(run_resident),
  check(run_twodisks),
  not(check(second_disk)),
  check(drive),
  cause(dirt).

diagnosed(floppy_disk) :-
  checkc(system,'2'),
  checkc(run,'8'),
  checkc(run_floppy_disk,'3'),
  check(run_floppy_physical),
  check(run_resident),
  check(run_twodisks),
  not(check(second_disk)),
  not(check(drive)),
  cause(bad_floppy_drive).

diagnosed(floppy_disk) :-
  checkc(system,'2'),
  checkc(run,'8'),
  checkc(run_floppy_disk,'3'),
  check(run_floppy_physical),
  check(run_resident),
  not(check(run_twodisks)),
  check(drive),
  cause(dirt).
```

```
diagnosed(floppy_disk) :-
  checkc(system,'2'),
  checkc(run,'8'),
  checkc(run_floppy_disk,'3'),
  check(run_floppy_physical),
  check(run_resident),
  not(check(run_twodisks)),
  not(check(drive)),
  check(run_disk_software),
  cause(run_disk_software).

diagnosed(floppy_disk) :-
  checkc(system,'2'),
  checkc(run,'8'),
  checkc(run_floppy_disk,'3'),
  check(run_floppy_physical),
  check(run_resident),
  not(check(run_twodisks)),
  not(check(drive)),
  not(check(run_disk_software)),
  check(run_one_floppy),
  cause(bad_floppy2).

diagnosed(floppy_disk) :-
  checkc(system,'2'),
  checkc(run,'8'),
  checkc(run_floppy_disk,'3'),
  check(run_floppy_physical),
  check(run_resident),
  not(check(run_twodisks)),
  not(check(drive)),
  not(check(run_disk_software)),
  not(check(run_one_floppy)),
  cause(bad_floppy_drive).

diagnosed(floppy_disk) :-
  checkc(system,'2'),
  checkc(run,'8'),
  checkc(run_floppy_disk,'4'),
  not(check(run_floppy_physical)),
  cause(run_floppy_physical).

diagnosed(floppy_disk) :-
  checkc(system,'2'),
  checkc(run,'8'),
  checkc(run_floppy_disk,'4'),
  check(run_floppy_physical),
  not(check(write_protect)),
  cause(write_protect).
```

Listing B.1 (cont.)

```
diagnosed(floppy_disk) :-
  checkc(system,'2'),
  checkc(run,'8'),
  checkc(run_floppy_disk,'4'),
  check(run_floppy_physical),
  check(write_protect),
  not(check(run_resident)),
  cause(run_resident).


diagnosed(floppy_disk) :-
  checkc(system,'2'),
  checkc(run,'8'),
  checkc(run_floppy_disk,'4'),
  check(run_floppy_physical),
  check(write_protect),
  check(run_resident),
  check(run_twodisks),
  check(second_disk),
  cause(bad_floppy).


diagnosed(floppy_disk) :-
  checkc(system,'2'),
  checkc(run,'8'),
  checkc(run_floppy_disk,'4'),
  check(run_floppy_physical),
  check(write_protect),
  check(run_resident),
  check(run_twodisks),
  not(check(second_disk)),
  check(drive),
  cause(dirt).


diagnosed(floppy_disk) :-
  checkc(system,'2'),
  checkc(run,'8'),
  checkc(run_floppy_disk,'4'),
  check(run_floppy_physical),
  check(write_protect),
  check(run_resident),
  check(run_twodisks),
  not(check(second_disk)),
  not(check(drive)),
  cause(bad_floppy_drive).
```

```
diagnosed(floppy_disk) :-
  checkc(system,'2'),
  checkc(run,'8'),
  checkc(run_floppy_disk,'4'),
  check(run_floppy_physical),
  check(write_protect),
  check(run_resident),
  not(check(run_twodisks)),
  check(drive),
  cause(dirt).

diagnosed(floppy_disk) :-
  checkc(system,'2'),
  checkc(run,'8'),
  checkc(run_floppy_disk,'4'),
  check(run_floppy_physical),
  check(write_protect),
  check(run_resident),
  not(check(run_twodisks)),
  not(check(drive)),
  check(run_disk_software),
  cause(run_disk_software).

diagnosed(floppy_disk) :-
  checkc(system,'2'),
  checkc(run,'8'),
  checkc(run_floppy_disk,'4'),
  check(run_floppy_physical),
  check(write_protect),
  check(run_resident),
  not(check(run_twodisks)),
  not(check(drive)),
  not(check(run_disk_software)),
  check(run_one_floppy),
  cause(bad_floppy2).

diagnosed(floppy_disk) :-
  checkc(system,'2'),
  checkc(run,'8'),
  checkc(run_floppy_disk,'4'),
  check(run_floppy_physical),
  check(write_protect),
  check(run_resident),
  not(check(run_twodisks)),
  not(check(drive)),
  not(check(run_disk_software)),
  not(check(run_one_floppy)),
  cause(bad_floppy_drive).
```

Listing B.1 (cont.)

```
diagnosed(floppy_disk) :-
  checkc(system,'2'),
  checkc(run,'8'),
  checkc(run_floppy_disk,'5'),
  not(check(run_floppy_physical)),
  cause(run_floppy_physical).

diagnosed(floppy_disk) :-
  checkc(system,'2'),
  checkc(run,'8'),
  checkc(run_floppy_disk,'5'),
  check(run_floppy_physical),
  cause(floppy_noise).

diagnosed(floppy_disk) :-
  checkc(system,'2'),
  checkc(run,'8'),
  checkc(run_floppy_disk,'6'),
  cause(floppy_load).

diagnosed(system_overheating) :-
  checkc(system,'2'),
  checkc(run,'9'),
  cause(run_overheating).

diagnosed(no_display) :-
  checkc(system,'3'),
  checkc(display,'1'),
  cause(no_display).

diagnosed(display_fade) :-
  checkc(system,'3'),
  checkc(display,'2'),
  cause(display_fade).

diagnosed(display_overheating) :-
  checkc(system,'3'),
  checkc(display,'3'),
  cause(display_overheating).

diagnosed(display_vertical) :-
  checkc(system,'3'),
  checkc(display,'4'),
  cause(display_vertical).
```

```
diagnosed(display_horizontal) :-
   checkc(system,'3'),
   checkc(display,'5'),
   cause(display_horizontal).


diagnosed(display_garbage) :-
   checkc(system,'3'),
   checkc(display,'6'),
   cause(display_garbage).


diagnosed(display_color) :-
   checkc(system,'3'),
   checkc(display,'7'),
   cause(display_color).


diagnosed(keyboard_dead) :-
   checkc(system,'4'),
   checkc(keyboard,'1'),
   cause(keyboard_dead).


diagnosed(keyboard_garbage) :-
   checkc(system,'4'),
   checkc(keyboard,'2'),
   cause(keyboard_garbage).


diagnosed(keyboard_keys) :-
   checkc(system,'4'),
   checkc(keyboard,'3'),
   cause(keyboard_keys).


diagnosed(keyboard_duplicates) :-
   checkc(system,'4'),
   checkc(keyboard,'4'),
   cause(keyboard_duplicates).


diagnosed(keyboard_foreign) :-
   checkc(system,'4'),
   checkc(keyboard,'5'),
   cause(keyboard_foreign).


diagnosed(keyboard_spill) :-
   checkc(system,'4'),
   checkc(keyboard,'6'),
   cause(keyboard_spill).
```

Listing B.1 (cont.)

```
diagnosed(printer_dead) :-
  checkc(system,'5'),
  checkc(printer,'a'),
  cause(printer_dead).

diagnosed(printer_notest) :-
  checkc(system,'5'),
  checkc(printer,'b'),
  cause(printer_notest).

diagnosed(printer_noline) :-
  checkc(system,'5'),
  checkc(printer,'c'),
  cause(printer_noline).

diagnosed(printer_junk) :-
  checkc(system,'5'),
  checkc(printer,'d'),
  not(check(printer_program)),
  cause(printer_junk).

diagnosed(printer_junk) :-
  checkc(system,'5'),
  checkc(printer,'d'),
  check(printer_program),
  cause(printer_program).

diagnosed(printer_erratic) :-
  checkc(system,'5'),
  checkc(printer,'e'),
  cause(printer_erratic).

diagnosed(printer_stops) :-
  checkc(system,'5'),
  checkc(printer,'f'),
  cause(printer_stops).

diagnosed(printer_carriage) :-
  checkc(system,'5'),
  checkc(printer,'g'),
  cause(printer_carriage).

diagnosed(printer_noprint) :-
  checkc(system,'5'),
  checkc(printer,'h'),
  cause(printer_noprint).
```

```
diagnosed(printer_overheat) :-
  checkc(system,'5'),
  checkc(printer,'i'),
  cause(printer_overheat).

diagnosed(printer_uneven) :-
  checkc(system,'5'),
  checkc(printer,'j'),
  cause(printer_uneven).

diagnosed(printer_missing) :-
  checkc(system,'5'),
  checkc(printer,'k'),
  cause(printer_missing).

diagnosed(printer_jams) :-
  checkc(system,'5'),
  checkc(printer,'l'),
  cause(paper_jams).

diag(floppy_disk_boot) :-
  checkc(floppy_boot,'1'),
  cause(drive_power).

diag(floppy_disk_boot) :-
  checkc(floppy_boot,'2'),
  check(physical_disk),nl,
  cause(physical_disk).

diag(floppy_disk_boot) :-
  checkc(floppy_boot,'2'),
  not(check(physical_disk)),nl,
  check(drive),
  cause(dirt).

diag(floppy_disk_boot) :-
  checkc(floppy_boot,'2'),
  not(check(physical_disk)),nl,
  not(check(drive)),
  check(twodisks),
  cause(twodisks).

diag(floppy_disk_boot) :-
  checkc(floppy_boot,'2'),
  not(check(physical_disk)),nl,
  not(check(drive)),
  not(check(twodisks)),
  cause(floppy_drive).
```

Listing B.1 (cont.)

```
diag(floppy_disk_boot) :-
  checkc(floppy_boot,'3'),
  cause(format).

diag(floppy_disk_boot) :-
  checkc(floppy_boot,'4'),
  cause(door).

diag(floppy_disk_boot) :-
  checkc(floppy_boot,'5'),
  cause(command).

check(X)  :-
  dbase(X,'y'),!.

check(X)  :-
  dbase(X,'n'),!,fail.

check(power) :-
  title,
  write("Check power cord, surge protector, and
      outlets."),nl,
  write("Is power getting to computer (y/n) ?"),
  response(Reply),
  asserta(dbase(power,Reply)),Reply='y'.

check(twodisks) :-
  title,
  write("Your next task is to isolate the problem
      between"),nl,
  write("the disk drive, controller, and disk cable.
      This is"),nl,
  write("simplified if you have a second disk drive in
      the unit"),nl,
  write("or a spare drive you can use."),nl,
  write("Do you have a spare or two floppy disk drives
      in the"),nl,
  write ("unit (y/n) ? "),
  response(Reply),
  asserta(dbase(twodisks,Reply)),Reply='y'.

check(memory) :-
  title,
  write("Does the memory test succeed (y/n) ? "),
  response(Reply),
  asserta(dbase(memory,Reply)),Reply='y'.
```

```
check(dos) :-
   title,
   write("Do you have DOS 2.0 or later installed on"),nl,
   write("the hard disk (y/n) ? "),
   response(Reply),
   asserta(dbase(dos,Reply)),Reply='y'.


check(hard_disk) :-
   title,
   write("Are you trying to boot from a hard disk (y/n) ?
      "),
   response(Reply),
   asserta(dbase(hard_disk,Reply)),Reply='y'.


check(hard) :-
   title,
   write("Touch the disk panel. Can you feel the motor
      turning "),nl,
   write("and does the load light on the disk flash"),nl,
   write("during boot (y/n) ? "),
   response(Reply),
   asserta(dbase(hard,Reply)),Reply='y'.


check(drive) :-
   title,
   write("Do a visual check of the drive. Be sure the
      disk "),nl,
   write("loads properly and the motor turns. Clean read
      head "),nl,
   write("using a head cleaning kit. Does it work now
      (y/n) ? "),
   response(Reply),
   asserta(dbase(drive,Reply)),Reply='y'.


check(floppy_disk_boot) :-
   title,
   write("Try to boot the system from a floppy disk.
      "),nl,
   write("Be sure it is a good disk with a good copy of
      DOS."),nl,
   write("Is this successful (y/n) ? "),nl,
   response(Reply),
   asserta(dbase(floppy_disk_boot,Reply)),Reply='y'.
```

Listing B.1 (cont.)

```prolog
check(physical_disk) :-
  title,
  write("Your next task is to isolate the problem to
     either "),nl,
  write("the physical disk or the hardware. Be sure the
     disk is"),nl,
  write("not physically damaged. Try other disks in the
     same"),nl,
  write("drive. Be sure the disk is formatted and
     contains DOS."),nl,
  write("Also, if possible, try to boot with this same
     disk on"),nl,
  write("another computer."),nl,
  write("Is the disk defective (y/n) ? "),
  response(Reply),
  asserta(dbase(physical_disk,Reply)),Reply='y'.

check(boot_read_hard) :-
  title,
  write("After booting from a floppy, try to read a
     directory "),nl,
  write("on the hard disk and start a program from the
     hard disk."),nl,
  write("Was this successful (y/n) ? "),
  response(Reply),
  asserta(dbase(boot_read_hard,Reply)),Reply='y'.

check(boot_write_hard) :-
  title,
  write("Try to restore DOS to the hard disk from a
     floppy "),nl,
  write("by putting a DOS disk in drive A and using SYS
     C:"),nl,
  write("Was this successful (y/n) ? "),
  response(Reply),
  asserta(dbase(boot_write_hard,Reply)),Reply='y'.

check(autoexec) :-
  title,
  write("Reboot from a floppy disk."),nl,
  write("Rename the AUTOEXEC.BAT file on the hard disk
     to"),nl,
  write("another name and try rebooting again from the
     "),nl,
  write("hard disk."),nl,
  write("Was this successful (y/n) ? "),
  response(Reply),
  asserta(dbase(autoexec,Reply)),Reply='y'.
```

Listing B.1 (cont.)

```prolog
check(config) :-
  title,
  write("Reboot from a floppy disk."),nl,
  write("Rename the CONFIG.SYS file on the hard
      disk"),nl,
  write("to another name. Try to boot again from the
      hard disk."),nl,
  write("Was this successful (y/n) ? "),
  response(Reply),
  asserta(dbase(config,Reply)),Reply='y'.


check(reboot) :-
  title,
  write("Try to get a successful reboot. Use"),nl,
  write("Alt/Ctrl/Del first. If it does not
      reboot,"),nl,
  write("turn the computer off and then on again."),nl,
  write("If this does not work, leave the computer off
      for"),nl,
  write("a while, then try to reboot again."),nl,
  write("Was the reboot eventually successful (y/n) ?
      "),
  response(Reply),
  asserta(dbase(reboot,Reply)),Reply='y'.


check(repeat) :-
  title,
  write("Try to repeat exactly what you did when
      the"),nl,
  write("computer locked up. Repeat each step exactly
      and"),nl,
  write("in the same order."),nl,
  write("Did the computer lock up again (y/n) ? "),
  response(Reply),
  asserta(dbase(repeat,Reply)),Reply='y'.


check(unplugged) :-
  title,
  write("Be sure the keyboard is plugged into the system
      and"),nl,
  write("no cables were inadvertently unplugged."),nl,
  write("Are all cables okay (y/n) ? "),
  response(Reply),
  asserta(dbase(unplugged,Reply)),Reply='y'.
```

Listing B.1 (cont.)

```
check(busy) :-
  title,
  write("Be sure the computer is not doing
      something"),nl,
  write("and the keyboard is purposely locked out
      until"),nl,
  write("this work has been completed. Watch disk
      lights."),nl,
  write("Is the computer really just busy (y/n) ? "),
  response(Reply),
  asserta(dbase(busy,Reply)),Reply='y'.


check(consistent) :-
  title,
  write("Is there anything consistent about the
      problem;"),nl,
  write("that is, does it always fail with the same
      program"),nl,
  write("when you do the same thing (y/n) ? "),
  response(Reply),
  asserta(dbase(consistent,Reply)),Reply='y'.


check(environment) :-
  title,
  write("Is the ambient temperature near the computer
      "),nl,
  write("<= 90 degrees Fahrenheit and >= 60
      degrees"),nl,
  write("Fahrenheit, all fans operational, and "),nl,
  write("all ventilation openings unblocked (y/n) ? "),
  response(Reply),
  asserta(dbase(environment,Reply)),Reply='y'.


check(run_program) :-
  title,
  write("Is this a DOS program (y/n) ? "),nl,
  response(Reply),
  asserta(dbase(run_program,Reply)),Reply='y'.


check(expansion) :-
  title,
  write("Is the hard disk in an expansion unit (y/n) ?
      "),
  response(Reply),
  asserta(dbase(expansion,Reply)),Reply='y'.
```

```
check(physical_move) :-
  title,
  write("Have you physically moved the hard disk
      recently (y/n) ? "),
  response(Reply),
  asserta(dbase(physical_move,Reply)),Reply='y'.


check(run_disk_software) :-
  title,
  write("Does this only happen with one program (y/n) ?
      "),
  response(Reply),
  asserta(dbase(run_disk_software,Reply)),Reply='y'.


check(run_resident) :-
  title,
  write("Try removing all resident programs by
      starting"),nl,
  write("without the AUTOEXEC.BAT file (RENAME it and
      reboot)."),nl,
  write("Does the problem persist (y/n) ? "),
  response(Reply),
  asserta(dbase(run_resident,Reply)),Reply='y'.


check(run_floppy_physical) :-
  title,
  write("Check the disk visually for physical
      damage."),nl,
  write("Does the disk appear okay (y/n) ? "),
  response(Reply),
  asserta(dbase(run_floppy_physical,Reply)),Reply='y'.


check(run_twodisks) :-
  title,
  write("Do you have a second disk drive or access"),nl,
  write("to another compatible computer (y/n) ? "),
  response(Reply),
  asserta(dbase(run_twodisks,Reply)),Reply='y'.


check(second_disk) :-
  title,
  write("Does the disk work the same way on the "),nl,
  write("other drive (y/n) ? "),
  response(Reply),
  asserta(dbase(second_disk,Reply)),Reply='y'.
```

Listing B.1 (cont.)

```
check(run_one_floppy) :-
  title,
  write("Does it always happen with one particular
      floppy"),nl,
  write("or with floppies of one brand (y/n) ?"),
  response(Reply),
  asserta(dbase(run_one_floppy,Reply)),Reply='y'.

check(write_protect) :-
  title,
  write("Is the write-protect hole on the disk uncovered
      (y/n) ?"),
  response(Reply),
  asserta(dbase(write_protect,Reply)),Reply='y'.

check(printer_program) :-
  title,
  write("Try to do a DIR list to the printer using"),nl,
  write("DIR, Ctrl/P, and Enter"),nl,
  write("Did this print correctly (y/n) ?"),
  response(Reply),
  asserta(dbase(printer_program,Reply)),Reply='y'.

check(one_beep) :-
  write("One short beep is the normal sound before
      system is"),nl,
  write("booted from the disk. If there is boot problem
      (y/n) ? "),
  response(Reply),Reply='y'.

checkc(Z,X) :-
  dbase(Z,Y),X=Y,!.

checkc(system,X) :-
  not(dbase(system,_)),
  repeat,
  title,
  write("What basic type of problem do you have? "),nl,
  write(" 1) Startup problem"),nl,
  write(" 2) Run problem"),nl,
  write(" 3) Display problem"),nl,
  write(" 4) Keyboard problem"),nl,
  write(" 5) Printer problem"),nl,
  write("SELECT: "),
  response(Reply),
  char_int(Reply,Z),
  Z<54,Z>48,!,
  asserta(dbase(system,Reply)),
  X=Reply.
```

```
checkc(startup,X) :-
  not(dbase(startup,_)),
  repeat,
  title,
  write("What type of startup problem do you have?
     "),nl,
  write(" 1) System errors during startup (POST
     fails)"),nl,
  write(" 2) Won't boot, no power light, nothing works,
     screen"),nl,
  write("      blank"),nl,
  write(" 3) Won't boot, power light on, nothing works,
     screen"),nl,
  write("      blank"),nl,
  write(" 4) POST works okay, no boot"),nl,
  write("SELECT: "),
  response(Reply),
  char_int(Reply,Z),
  Z<53,Z>48,!,
  asserta(dbase(startup,Reply)),
  X=Reply.
```

Listing B.1 (cont.)

```
checkc(beep,X) :-
  not(dbase(beep,_)),
  repeat,
  title,
  write("How many beeps do you hear when the "),nl,
  write("initial diagnostics run? "),nl,
  write("     1) There is no beep and nothing
     happens."),nl,
  write("     2) There is one short beep and the disk
     light"),nl,
  write("  comes on."),nl,
  write("     3) There is one continuous beep."),nl,
  write("     4) There is one long and one short
     beep."),nl,
  write("     5) There is one long and two short
     beeps."),nl,
  write("     6) There is one short beep and a blank or
     incorrect"),nl,
  write("  display."),nl,
  write("     7) There is a repeating short beep."),nl,
  write("     8) One short beep and BASIC OK
     prompt."),nl,
  write("SELECT: "),
  response(Reply),
  char_int(Reply,Z),
  Z<57,Z>48,!,
  asserta(dbase(beep,Reply)),
  X=Reply.
```

Listing B.1 (cont.)

```
checkc(errorcode,X) :-
  not(dbase(errorcode,_)),
  repeat,
  title,
  write("If an error message is displayed, what is the
    "),nl,
  write("message? "),nl,
  write("       a) (no error message displayed)"),nl,
  write("       b) 101 or 131 or 1xx"),nl,
  write("       c) 201 or xxxx201 Parity Check x or 20x or
    xx20x"),nl,
  write("       d) 301 or xx301 or Keyboard not functional
    or 30x or"),nl,
  write("  xx30x"),nl,
  write("       e) 601 or 6xx"),nl,
  write("       f) 4xx"),nl,
  write("       g) 5xx"),nl,
  write("       h) 9xx"),nl,
  write("       i) 13xx"),nl,
  write("       j) 14xx or Printer Problems"),nl,
  write("       k) 1701 or 17xx"),nl,
  write("       l) 1801 or 18xx"),nl,
  write("       m) 02x"),nl,
  write("SELECT: "),
  response(Reply),
  char_int(Reply,Z),
  Z<110,Z>96,!,
  asserta(dbase(errorcode,Reply)),
  X=Reply.
```

Listing B.1 (cont.)

```
checkc(floppy_boot,X) :-
  not(dbase(floppy_boot,_)),
  repeat,
  title,
  write("Your next strategy should be to try to
      diagnose"),nl,
  write("the problem with the floppy disk boot,
      deciding"),nl,
  write("if the problem is the disk or computer
      system."),
  write("What are the disk drive symptoms? "),nl,
  write("    1) The floppy disk drive is dead--no
      load"),nl,
  write("  light or motor (feel panel) during
      boot."),nl,
  write("    2) The load light comes on and the motor
      turns,"),nl,
  write("  but nothing else happens."),nl,
  write("    3) You get the message 'Non-system disk
      or"),nl,
  write("  disk error' or the message 'Disk boot"),nl,
  write("  failure'."),nl,
  write("    4) You get a 'Drive not ready' error
      message."),nl,
  write("    5) You get the message 'Bad or missing
      Command"),nl,
  write("  interpreter'."),nl,
  write("SELECT: "),
  response(Reply),
  char_int(Reply,Z),
  Z<54,Z>48,!,
  asserta(dbase(floppy_boot,Reply)),
  X=Reply.
```

```
checkc(run_hard_disk,X) :-
    not(dbase(run_hard_disk,_)),
    repeat,
    title,
    write("What are the hard disk symptoms? "),nl,
    write("      1) The hard disk is dead--no load
        light"),nl,
    write("  when accessed."),nl,
    write("      2) Does not read or write properly."),nl,
    write("      3) Reads correctly, but does not
        write."),nl,
    write("      4) CHKDSK program generates error
        messages."),nl,
    write("      5) The disk makes an unusual sound."),nl,
    write("      6) Disk lost information previously
        stored."),nl,
    write("SELECT: "),
    response(Reply),
    char_int(Reply,Z),
    Z<55,Z>48,!,
    asserta(dbase(run_hard_disk,Reply)),
    X=Reply.

checkc(run_floppy_disk,X) :-
    not(dbase(run_floppy_disk,_)),
    repeat,
    title,
    write("What are the disk symptoms? "),nl,
    write("      1) The floppy disk is dead--no load
        light"),nl,
    write("  when accessed."),nl,
    write("      2) The following message is
        displayed:"),nl,
    write("   'Not ready reading drive X"),nl,
    write("    Abort, Retry, Ignore?'"),nl,
    write("      3) Does not read or write properly."),nl,
    write("      4) Reads correctly, but does not
        write."),nl,
    write("      5) The disk makes an unusual sound."),nl,
    write("      6) Difficult to load or unload
        disks."),nl,
    write("SELECT: "),
    response(Reply),
    char_int(Reply,Z),
    Z<55,Z>48,!,
    asserta(dbase(run_floppy_disk,Reply)),
    X=Reply.
```

Listing B.1 (cont.)

```
checkc(run,X) :-
  not(dbase(run,_)),
  repeat,
  title,
  write("What type of run problem are you experiencing?
    "),nl,
  write("      1) Computer locks up but power stays
    up,"),nl,
  write("  keyboard is dead."),nl,
  write("      2) Computer drops power, turning itself
    off. "),nl,
  write("      3) Parity error messages."),nl,
  write("      4) Computer crashes when turning on
    peripheral."),nl,
  write("      5) Erratic operation or intermittent
    failures."),nl,
  write("      6) Problems in operating one specific
    program."),nl,
  write("      7) Hard disk problems."),nl,
  write("      8) Floppy disk problems."),nl,
  write("      9) Overheating"),nl,
  write("SELECT: "),
  response(Reply),
  char_int(Reply,Z),
  Z<58,Z>48,!,
  asserta(dbase(run,Reply)),
  X=Reply.
```

Listing B.1 (cont.)

```
checkc(display,X) :-
  not(dbase(display,_)),
  repeat,
  title,
  write("What type of display problem are you
     experiencing? "),nl,
  write("     1) There is no display."),nl,
  write("     2) The display fades in and out."),nl,
  write("     3) The monitor is overheating."),nl,
  write("     4) There is no vertical
     synchronization."),nl,
  write("     5) There is no horizontal
     synchronization."),nl,
  write("     6) Garbage is displayed."),nl,
  write("     7) Bad or no color on color monitor."),nl,
  write("SELECT: "),
  response(Reply),
  char_int(Reply,Z),
  Z<56,Z>48,!,
  asserta(dbase(display,Reply)),
  X=Reply.
```

Listing B.1 (cont.)

```
checkc(keyboard,X) :-
  not(dbase(keyboard,_)),
  repeat,
  title,
  write("Be sure, before continuing, that you have
      not"),nl,
  write("physically damaged the keyboard. If you
      have"),nl,
  write("spilled coffee on the keyboard, for example,
      seek"),nl,
  write("more professional help."),nl,
  write("What type of keyboard problem are you
      experiencing? "),nl,
  write("    1) Keyboard does not do anything."),nl,
  write("    2) Keyboard prints wrong characters."),nl,
  write("    3) One or more keys don't work."),nl,
  write("    4) When you press a key, two or more
      characters"),nl,
  write("  appear."),nl,
  write("    5) A foreign object was dropped into the
      keyboard."),nl,
  write("    6) Something was spilled on the
      keyboard."),nl,
  write("SELECT: "),
  response(Reply),
  char_int(Reply,Z),
  Z<56,Z>48,!,
  asserta(dbase(keyboard,Reply)),
  X=Reply.
```

```
checkc(printer,X) :-
  not(dbase(printer,_)),
  repeat,
  title,
  write("What type of printer problem are you
      experiencing? "),nl,
  write("      a) Printer is dead."),nl,
  write("      b) Printer will not do self-test. (See
      "),nl,
  write("  printer manual)."),nl,
  write("      c) Self-test works, but printer fails
      online."),nl,
  write("      d) Printer prints garbage."),nl,
  write("      e) Printer has erratic, occasional
      errors."),nl,
  write("      f) Printer suddenly stops while
      printing."),nl,
  write("      g) Carriage freezes up and does not
      move."),nl,
  write("      h) Printer runs fine, but does not
      print"),nl,
  write("  anything."),nl,
  write("      i) Printer or print head overheats."),nl,
  write("      j) Characters are printed unevenly."),nl,
  write("      k) Part of printed characters are
      missing."),nl,
  write("      l) The paper jams."),nl,
  write("SELECT: "),
  response(Reply),
  char_int(Reply,Z),
  Z<109,Z>96,!,
  asserta(dbase(printer,Reply)),
  X=Reply.

response(Reply) :-
  readchar(Reply),
  write(Reply),nl.

cause(ac_power) :-
  write("Probable cause is loss of ac power."),nl,
  write("Check to be sure power cable is plugged into
      system"),nl,
  write("unit and wall. Be sure power is at wall outlet
      (no fuse out).").
```

Listing B.1 (cont.)

```
cause(switch) :-
  write("Probable cause is on/off switch or power
    supply."),nl,
  write("Check on/off switch on system unit and internal
    "),nl,
  write("power supply.").


cause(no_power) :-
  write("Probable defective power supply or power
    supply"),nl,
  write("connectors. Check internal power supply
    cables."),nl,
  write("Check microprocessor chip and ROM chip."),nl,
  write("Possible system board problem.").


cause(power_supply) :-
  write("Probable defective internal power supply."),nl,
  write("Check power supply and internal power supply
    cables.").


cause(system_board) :-
  write("You have a defective system board. Repair or
    replace.").


cause(system_board2) :-
  write("The system board switches are set wrong
    or"),nl,
  write("you have a defective system board. Check
    switches"),
  write("or replace system board.").


cause(display) :-
  write("You have a defective display or display
    cable."),nl,
  write("Replace or repair.").


cause(disk_drive) :-
  write("You have a defective or disconnected floppy
    disk drive,"),nl,
  write("drive cable, or disk drive controller."),nl,
  write("Replace or connect the drive and controller.").
```

Listing B.1 (cont.)

```
cause(memory) :-
    write("There is one or more defective memory chips in
        the"),nl,
    write("system board or an adapter board. Be sure all
        memory"),nl,
    write("chips are firmly seated in their sockets and no
        pins"),nl,
    write("are outside of sockets. Use a diagnostic, if
        necessary,"),nl,
    write("to locate the specific chip at fault.").


cause(keyboard) :-
    write("The keyboard is not connected or is
        defective."),nl,
    write("Connect keyboard or replace.").


cause(mono_monitor) :-
    write("The monochrome monitor is not connected or is
        defective."),nl,
    write("Check monitor, adapter card, and monitor
        cables. ").


cause(color_monitor) :-
    write("The color monitor is not connected or is
        defective."),nl,
    write("Check monitor, adapter card, and monitor
        cables. ").


cause(printer) :-
    write("The printer is not connected or is
        defective."),nl,
    write("Check printer, printer adapter card, and
        cables. ").


cause(hard_disk) :-
    write("You have a defective or disconnected hard disk.
        "),nl,
    write("Check disk controller card, disk, and power to
        disk.").


cause(game_adapter) :-
    write("The game adapter is not connected or is
        defective."),nl,
    write("Check game adapter, game adapter card, and
        cables. ").
```

Listing B.1 (cont.)

```
cause(expansion_unit) :-
   write("You have a defective or disconnected expansion
      unit. "),nl,
   write("Check to be sure expansion unit is connected
      and"),nl,
   write("turned on. If everything is on and connected,
      check"),nl,
   write("for a defective cable or expansion unit. You
      should"),nl,
   write("still be able to boot from a floppy disk drive
      or any"),nl,
   write("hard disk in the main unit.").


cause(config) :-
   write("Something in the CONFIG.SYS file is preventing
      the"),nl,
   write("completion of the boot. Be particularly
      suspicious"),nl,
   write("of anything added recently to the file. Also
      be"),nl,
   write("suspicious of any DEVICE= lines. There may be a
      "),nl,
   write("hardware or software driver problem with one
      of"),nl,
   write("these devices.").


cause(hard_disk) :-
   write("The hard disk or disk controller is defective,
      or"),nl,
   write("possibly no power to hard disk drive. If drive
      is in"),nl,
   write("expansion unit, be sure it is on and power
      supply is"),nl,
   write("working.").


cause(dos) :-
   write("Install a DOS 2.0 or later on the hard disk.").


cause(boot_read_hard) :-
   write("If you cannot read the directory on the hard
      disk, you"),nl,
   write("have probably lost data and programs on the
      disk. Try "),nl,
   write("to reformat the hard disk and restore from a
      backup.").
```

Listing B.1 (cont.)

```prolog
cause(bad_dos) :-
    write("You had a defective DOS on the hard disk.").

cause(autoexec) :-
    write("Something in the AUTOEXEC.BAT file is
        preventing the"),nl,
    write("completion of the boot. Be particularly
        suspicious"),nl,
    write("of anything added recently to the file.").

cause(unknown) :-
    write("I am having a problem isolating the problem.
        "),nl,
    write("Be particularly suspicious of any new
        hardware"),nl,
    write("or software installed, removing it and
        trying"),nl,
    write("the boot again. Check switches on the system
        board."),nl.

cause(drive_power) :-
    write("Drive is defective, or there is no power to"),
    write("drive. Check power supply, and power cable to
        drive."),nl,
    write("If drive has power, replace or repair drive.").

cause(physical_disk) :-
    write("If the floppy disk is physically damaged,
        destroy it"),nl,
    write("after being sure you have a backup.").

cause(dirt) :-
    write("Problem was probably a dirty read head or
        other"),nl,
    write("foreign matter in the drive. Try to keep
        disk"),nl,
    write("environment clean.").
```

Listing B.1 (cont.)

```
cause(twodisks) :-
  write("First, try to boot on the other disk drive, if
      your"),nl,
  write("computer permits this. If you can boot from the
      other"),nl,
  write("drive, the drive is probably at fault."),nl,
  write("Check for broken or loose drive belt. "),nl,
  write("If you can't boot, you may have controller
      or"),nl,
  write("cable problems."),nl,
  write("Alternately, you can make drive B into drive A
      by "),nl,
  write("swapping the two plug-in modules on the disk
      drive"),nl,
  write("electronic card near where the disk cable
      connects"),nl,
  write("from the controller. If you can't boot on the
      new"),nl,
  write("drive A, suspect controller or cable
      problems."),nl,
  write("If you can boot, suspect drive problems.
      "),nl,
  write("Drive problems are most likely bad belt, motor,
      or"),nl,
  write("bad alignment.").

cause(floppy_drive) :-
  write("Apparent problem is the disk drive, internal
      drive"),nl,
  write("cable, or controller. Be sure disk drive belt
      is not"),nl,
  write("broken and motor is turning when load light is
      on. "),nl,
  write("Isolate cause by swapping out drive,
      controller, and"),nl,
  write("cable--one at a time.").

cause(format) :-
  write("The disk is not formatted properly or does not
      have"),nl,
  write("DOS on it. Use a formatted disk with DOS on
      it."),nl,
  write("The problem was a disk problem.").
```

```
cause(door) :-
  write("The disk is not formatted properly or the"),nl,
  write("drive door was open."),nl,
  write("Close door or replace disk.").


cause(command) :-
  write("The COMMAND.COM file is not on the disk."),nl,
  write("Use a DOS disk with a COMMAND.COM file.").


cause(unplugged) :-
  write("Reroute or change cables to protect
     against"),nl,
  write("the problem again.").


cause(hardware) :-
  write("First, try to boot from a floppy disk to
     check"),nl,
  write("for bad DOS. If this does not work, repeat
     this"),nl,
  write("consultation checking for boot problems."),nl,
  write("The problem is most likely a defective
     system"),nl,
  write("board, bad keyboard, or a bad memory
     chip."),nl,
  write("Substitute a good keyboard to check the
     keyboard."),nl.


cause(software) :-
  write("Check for a problem with the particular program
     you"),nl,
  write("are running. Remove all resident programs and
     try"),nl,
  write("the steps again. You may have a conflict with a
     "),nl,
  write("resident program. If the program is new and
     uses special "),nl,
  write("hardware, there may be an interrupt conflict.
     See"),nl,
  write("the DOS technical manual for how the interrupts
     are "),nl,
  write("used and identify how you are using them on
     your "),nl,
  write("computer.").
```

Listing B.1 (cont.)

```
cause(static) :-
  write("The problem was probably caused by static
    electricity"),nl,
  write("or a power line surge. Be sure you are using a
    surge"),nl,
  write("protector to protect against future surges.
    Static mats"),nl,
  write("and special antistatic sprays can prevent
    static problems.").


cause(busy) :-
  write("Many programs purposely lock up the keyboard
    during "),nl,
  write("execution to prevent the user from changing
    data"),nl,
  write("when it should not be changed. If this is a
    problem for"),nl,
  write("you, get a faster computer or one that
    supports"),nl,
  write("multiple program execution (multitasking).").


cause(drop_power) :-
  write("The most likely cause is a power surge,
    static"),nl,
  write("electricity, defective power supply, or a bad
    system board."),nl,
  write("Install a surge protector if you do not have
    one. Add"),nl,
  write("a static mat if necessary. If this does not
    work, check"),nl,
  write("the power supply, then the system board.").


cause(parity_error) :-
  write("The most general cause is a memory chip
    failure. This "),nl,
  write("chip can be located with a good memory
    diagnostic. "),nl,
  write("Another cause, however, can be any hardware
    that "),nl,
  write("uses the parity error interrupt, such as some
    EGA"),nl,
  write("boards. If you recently installed some new
    hardware"),nl,
  write("or software, be suspicious of it creating the
    parity"),nl,
  write("error interrupt message.").
```

```
cause(crashes) :-
  write("The most likely causes would be: (1) A software
      bug in"),nl,
  write("a particular program. (2) A problem in a
      hardware or "),nl,
  write("software driver. (3) System board or power
      supply problem.").

cause(erratic_software) :-
  write("Check for conflicts with resident programs. If
      there are"),nl,
  write("no conflicts, try creating a new copy of the
      program"),nl,
  write("from the master. Check with the program
      manufacturer"),nl,
  write("if the problem persists.").

cause(environment) :-
  write("The air temperature near the computer should be
      no more"),nl,
  write("than 90 degrees Fahrenheit and no less than 60
      degrees"),nl,
  write("Fahrenheit. This can vary with products--check
      with your"),nl,
  write("computer manufacturer.").

cause(run_hard_disk) :-
  write("There is a defective power cable or the hard
      disk"),nl,
  write("drive is defective.").

cause(run_expansion) :-
  write("Be sure expansion unit is on. If on, the power
      supply,"),nl,
  write("the power supply cable, or the hard disk is
      defective.").

cause(run_harddisk_write) :-
  write("The problem is a bad drive, bad controller
      card, or"),nl,
  write("bad controller-to-drive cable.").

cause(run_harddisk_read) :-
  write("The problem is a bad drive, bad controller
      card, or"),nl,
  write("bad controller-to-drive cable.").
```

Listing B.1 (cont.)

```
cause(run_harddisk_chkdsk) :-
  write("The problem could be caused by defective disk
      drive."),nl,
  write("Often, however, this is caused by a poorly
      designed"),nl,
  write("application program. If CHKDSK is able to
      find"),nl,
  write("lost clusters after running an old program,
      suspect"),nl,
  write("the cause to be the old program. New programs
      (1985-) take"),nl,
  write("advantage of newer DOS functions that eliminate
      the problem.").


cause(run_harddisk_noisy) :-
  write("The most likely cause is a bearing going out
      on"),nl,
  write("the drive. Back up the disk immediately, then
      have"),nl,
  write("the disk checked.").


cause(run_hard) :-
  write("Suspect the drive is going bad. BACK UP DISK
      IMMEDIATELY!"),nl,
  write("Have disk checked after backing it up.").


cause(physical_move) :-
  write("On many computers, the disk drive head must be
      'parked'"),nl,
  write("before the disk is moved. This is done using an
      option"),nl,
  write("on the diagnostic disk. If necessary on your
      system, "),nl,
  write("always park head before moving. Rewrite bad
      data or "),nl,
  write("programs to disk from backups to recover this
      time.").


cause(run_disk_software) :-
  write("Some programs may have difficulties working
      with some"),nl,
  write("disks. If the problem is with a single program,
      "),nl,
  write("check with the program manufacturer.").
```

223

Listing B.1 (cont.)

```
cause(run_resident) :-
  write("Some resident software can interfere with
      reading and"),nl,
  write("writing to the disk. Try removing specific
      resident"),nl,
  write("programs or installing them in a different
      order.").


cause(run_floppy_physical) :-
  write("Recover whatever data you can from the disk,
      then"),nl,
  write("destroy the disk. ").


cause(bad_floppy) :-
  write("Recover the data you can from the disk, then
      reformat"),nl,
  write("the disk and test it. If it fails again,
      destroy the"),nl,
  write("disk or replace it. You should probably change
      disk"),nl,
  write("brands if this happens with several disks of
      the same brand.").


cause(bad_floppy_drive) :-
  write("The problem is most likely a bad floppy drive
      or "),nl,
  write("a need for a drive alignment. If the problem
      occurs"),nl,
  write("frequently, have the drive repaired.").


cause(bad_floppy2) :-
  write("If it consistently happens with the same disk,
      "),nl,
  write("backup and then destroy or replace the disk.
      If"),nl,
  write("it consistently happens with several disks of
      one"),nl,
  write("brand, switch to another brand.").


cause(run_floppy_disk_power) :-
  write("Probable cause is bad disk power cable or power
      supply.").
```

Listing B.1 (cont.)

```
cause(run_floppy_not_ready) :-
  write("Most probable cause is disk inserted wrong
      or"),nl,
  write("disk door open. This can also be caused by a
      "),nl,
  write("defective disk or by trying to read a disk that
      "),nl,
  write("is not formatted. Try the disk on another drive
      or"),nl,
  write("computer. If it works, suspect broken drive
      belt"),nl,
  write("or defective drive.").


cause(write_protect) :-
  write("You cannot write to the disk unless the hole on
      the"),nl,
  write("outside edge of the disk is uncovered.").


cause(floppy_noise) :-
  write("Probable cause is broken drive belt in drive,
      a"),nl,
  write("foreign object in drive, or defective drive
      motor.").


cause(floppy_load) :-
  write("Probable cause is foreign object in drive,
      latch"),nl,
  write("problem, or loose part.").


cause(run_overheating) :-
  write("The probable cause is a defective fan, or
      blocked"),nl,
  write("fan vent or input ventilation holes. Be sure
      fan turns"),nl,
  write("and clean fan filter if necessary. Be sure you
      are not"),nl,
  write("putting too many or too power-intensive adapter
      cards"),nl,
  write("in the system.").


cause(run_software_dos) :-
  write("Look up the error message in the DOS
      manual"),nl,
  write("and follow the suggested procedure.").
```

```
cause(run_software_application) :-
  write("Contact the software company by letter or
     phone"),nl,
  write("for help. Document now exactly what you were
     doing"),nl,
  write("when it happened and try the procedure again
     to"),nl,
  write("determine whether it is an isolated incident
     or"),nl,
  write("verifiable and repeatable.").

cause(no_display) :-
  write("Be sure monitor has power and is on. Be sure
     "),nl,
  write("brightness control is turned up. Check for
     defective"),nl,
  write("video cable or monitor.").

cause(display_fade) :-
  write("Power may be defective--substitute another
     monitor"),nl,
  write("to test this. If fault is with monitor, it is
     defective.").

cause(display_overheating) :-
  write("Be sure nothing is blocking monitor
     ventilation. "),nl,
  write("Monitor may be defective.").

cause(display_vertical) :-
  write("Adjust vertical hold. You may also have a
     defective"),nl,
  write("monitor or adapter card.").

cause(display_horizontal) :-
  write("Adjust horizontal hold. You may also have a
     defective"),nl,
  write("monitor or adapter card.").
```

Listing B.1 (cont.)

```
cause(display_garbage) :-
  write("Be sure it is not the keyboard. If the keyboard
     is"),nl,
  write("bad, the display will be all right during boot,
     but "),nl,
  write("wrong characters displayed when entered from
     the keyboard. Because"),nl,
  write("the screen 'image' is always displayed from an
     area of"),nl,
  write("computer memory, this memory may be bad or the
     adapter"),nl,
  write("that sends it to the monitor may be bad. ").

cause(display_color) :-
  write("Be sure the color controls are adjusted
     properly."),nl,
  write("If controls are working, problem is probably
     "),nl,
  write("adapter card.").

cause(keyboard_dead) :-
  write("Be sure first that it really is the keyboard--
     even"),nl,
  write("if the keyboard is bad, the computer should
     boot and"),nl,
  write("the display should show the proper starting
     messages. If"),nl,
  write("the display is fine on starting, check for bad
     keyboard"),nl,
  write("cable, bad keyboard (substitute a good one), or
     bad "),nl,
  write("system board.").

cause(keyboard_garbage) :-
  write("Be sure there is no stuck key. Be sure it is
     the "),nl,
  write("keyboard--characters on display should be right
     "),nl,
  write("on starting. If there is no stuck key,
     suspect"),nl,
  write("defective keyboard (substitute a good one to
     check).").
```

```
cause(keyboard_keys) :-
  write("Purchase a can of pressurized air at a photo
     store."),nl,
  write("Remove power from keyboard."),nl,
  write("Blow air under keys to clear out any debris.
     Use"),nl,
  write("screwdriver to gently remove cap of offending
     key."),nl,
  write("Use electronic contact cleaner to clear key
     switch."),nl,
  write("Replace cap. If this fails, suspect keyboard
     electronics.").

cause(keyboard_duplicates) :-
  write("Reboot first. A bad boot can cause this type of
     "),nl,
  write("operation. Duplication is normal if the key is
     held"),nl,
  write("down for a few seconds. If this does not stop
     it:"),nl,
  write("Purchase a can of pressurized air at a photo
     store."),nl,
  write("Remove power from keyboard."),nl,
  write("Blow air under keys to clear out any debris.
     Use"),nl,
  write("screwdriver to gently remove cap of offending
     key."),nl,
  write("Use electronic contact cleaner to clear key
     switch."),nl,
  write("Replace cap. If this fails, suspect keyboard
     electronics.").

cause(keyboard_foreign) :-
  write("Purchase a can of pressurized air at a photo
     store."),nl,
  write("Remove power from keyboard."),nl,
  write("Blow air under keys to clear out any debris.
     Use"),nl,
  write("screwdriver to gently remove cap of offending
     key."),nl,
  write("Use electronic contact cleaner to clear key
     switch."),nl,
  write("Replace cap. If this fails, suspect keyboard
     electronics.").
```

Listing B.1 (cont.)

```prolog
cause(keyboard_spill) :-
  write("Remove power from keyboard IMMEDIATELY!"),nl,
  write("Soak up what you can with a rag."),nl,
  write("Use canned pressurized air (photo store) to
      remove"),nl,
  write("what you can. Leave keyboard 48 hours to
      dry."),nl,
  write("Check out. It may or may not need more
      repair.").

cause(printer_dead) :-
  write("Defective printer power supply, fuse blown, or
      no"),nl,
  write("voltage to printer.").

cause(printer_notest) :-
  write("Printer is defective. ").

cause(printer_noline) :-
  write("Defective cable to printer or printer
      adapter"),nl,
  write("card.").

cause(printer_junk) :-
  write("Baud rate switch on printer not set right or
      other"),nl,
  write("printer switches not set right.").

cause(printer_program) :-
  write("Program printer driver not selected properly.
      Select"),nl,
  write("the proper driver in the program. Call program
      "),nl,
  write("manufacturer if necessary.").

cause(printer_erratic) :-
  write("Printer not adjusted correctly, bad cable, or
      dust"),nl,
  write("in printer. ").

cause(printer_stops) :-
  write("No ribbon, no paper, or printer jammed. If
      these are okay, try"),nl,
  write("printer self-test. If self-test works, check
      cable"),nl,
  write("and printer adapter card.").
```

Listing B.1 (cont.)

```prolog
cause(printer_carriage) :-
  write("Turn off power. Check for foreign object
     jamming"),nl,
  write("printer. Check carriage movement. ").

cause(printer_noprint) :-
  write("Ribbon not installed correctly or ribbon jumped
     out"),nl,
  write("of position. If ribbon is correct, print head
     may be"),nl,
  write("defective.").

cause(printer_overheat) :-
  write("Print head jammed or ventilation blocked.").

cause(printer_missing) :-
  write("If print wheel is used (daisy-wheel
     printer),"),nl,
  write("check for defective wheel. If dot-matrix
     printer,"),nl,
  write("check for defective print head."),nl,
  write("Check for dirty printer hammer or head."),nl,
  write("If clean, have printer alignment checked. ").

cause(paper_jams) :-
  write("Wrong type of paper or paper is not loaded
     correctly."),nl,
  write("Check paper path. Be sure there are no
     foreign"),nl,
  write("objects in path.").

  cause(printer_uneven) :-
  write("Printer needs adjustment.").
```

Appendix C

Answers to Exercises

Chapter 1

1. Not applicable

2. A knowledge engineer and a programmer approach a problem from different perspectives. A programmer defines—in a very detailed manner—how to get from A to B. A knowledge engineer, in contrast, visualizes the relationships between facts and chunks these relationships into a meaningful database. In short, the programmer is good at developing algorithms, the knowledge engineer at developing heuristics. Both have skills in formal and numerical reasoning and the ability to define clear and objective goals.

3. Selections a and d are generally procedural systems if built with today's technology. All involve numerical processing, and an expert system approach would probably be too slow or very costly. Applications c and e would most likely be done with an expert system today. Applications b and f are borderline, and the decision would depend on the objective and the financial resources available.

Chapter 2

1a. Procedural
1b. Procedural

1c. Declarative

1d. Declarative

1e. Can be used either way, but is generally procedural

1f. Procedural

1g. Procedural

1h. Declarative

1i. Procedural

2. Prolog requires extensive memory for adequate speed, and works best with parallel architectures. It is also primarily limited to backward depth-first reasoning. Another disadvantage is the lack of a good standard. Prolog will become more accepted as memory and processors drop in cost and the language matures.

3. Prolog is relatively easy to learn because it is a natural language; that is, it mimics the way a human thinks. Some aspects of Prolog, such as the cut, are difficult to learn because of the "unnatural" aspect of the specific feature—not because the feature is nonprocedural.

Chapter 3

Not applicable

Chapter 4

1a. Nonvalid

1b. String

1c. String

1d. Nonvalid

1e. Integer

1f. Symbol

1g. Symbol

1h. Character

1i. Symbol

1j. Nonvalid

1k. Symbol (This is valid, but should not be used because of possible confusion with the built-in predicate.)

2. Selection e is not valid. Selections a, b, c, and d are valid. But to prevent confusion with the built-in predicate, b should not be used.

3. Selections c and e are variable names; a, b, and d are object names.

Chapter 5

1. The goal succeeds with:

```
        X=battery_charged
```

2. Not applicable

Chapter 6

1. To add password control:

```
go :-
  write("Please enter your password: "),
  readln(Password),nl,
  password(Password),
  (program).

go :-
  write("Sorry, you are not permitted
    access."),nl.

password("Superman").
password("Bigfoot").
```

2. Not applicable

Chapter 7

1. By using the string type, the object names can include spaces, commas, and other special characters.

2. Not applicable

3. Modify the first *run* predicate as follows:

```
run:-
  write("AUTOMOBILE DIAGNOSTIC SYSTEM"),nl,
  diagnosed(_),!,nl,save("test.dat"),clear_fact
```

Chapter 8

1. The following is displayed:

```
BEGIN
Thisisatest TRY AGAIN
Thisisatest
END OF DATA
End of test 2True
```

2. The output is:

```
BEGIN
This
```

```
                              END
                              True
```

3. Not applicable

Chapter 9

1. Lists can represent practically any type of structure used in symbolic computation. They are dynamic structures; that is, their length can change during program execution. List capability exists in very few languages. It is limited primarily to Prolog, LISP, and FORTH. Lists can be used to parse sentences, build ordered hierarchies (for example, biological, geographical, and organizational), and work with collections of data as a single unit (such as addresses and inventories).

2a. Head: 85
   Tail: [96,75,87,94,98,91]

2b. Head: blue
   Tail: [red,black,green,white]

2c. Head: bob
   Tail: [sue,mary,bill]

3a. [85¦[96,75,87,94,98,91]]

3b. [blue ¦ [red,black,green,white]]

3c. [bob ¦[sue,mary,bill]]

4. Not applicable

5. The program is:

```
domains
  person=address(name,street,city,state,zip)
  name,street,city,state,zip = string

database
  xaddress(person)

predicates
readaddress(person)
run

clauses
run :-
  consult("address.dat"),
  readaddress(Address),nl,
  asserta(xaddress(Address)),
  save("address.dat"),!.

readaddress(address(Name,Street,City,
  State,Zip)) :-
```

```
            write("Name: "),readln(Name),
            write("Address: " ),readln(Street),
            write("City: "),readln(City),
            write("State: "),readln(State),
            write("Zip: "),readln(Zip).
```

Chapter 10

1. The logon routine is:

```
domains
  name,password = symbol

predicates
  getinput(name,password)
  logon(integer)
  user(name,password)
  run

clauses
  run :-
    logon(3),
    write("You are now logged on."),nl.

  logon(0) :- !,fail.

  logon(_) :-
    getinput(Name,Password),
    user(Name,Password).

  logon(N) :-
    write("Sorry, you are not allowed
      access."),nl,
    NN=N-1,
    logon(NN).

  getinput(Name,Password) :-
    write("Please enter your name: "),
    readln(Name),nl,
    write("Please enter your password: "),
    readln(Password),nl.

  user(joe,superglue).
  user(melody,pink_lady).
  user(sue,smartstuff).
```

2. Add the predicate:

```
            domains
              delay(integer)

            clauses
              delay(0) :- !.
              delay(N) :-
                NN = N - 1,
                delay(NN).
```

Modify the first *run* predicate as follows:

```
            run:-
              delay(55),
              write("AUTOMOBILE DIAGNOSTIC SYSTEM")
              ,nl,
              diagnosed(_),!,nl,clear_facts.
```

Set the value of the argument in the previous delay predicate to get the desired delay.

Chapter 11

1. Add the goal section as follows:

```
            /*      AUTOMOTIVE DIAGNOSTIC SYSTEM
                       with internal goal
            /*

            database
              xpositive(symbol)
              xnegative(symbol)

            predicates
              run
              diagnosed(symbol)
              check(symbol)
              positive(string,symbol)
              negative(string,symbol)
              clear_facts
              remember(symbol,char)
              ask(string,symbol,char)

            goal
              run.

            clauses
              run:-
                write("AUTOMOBILE DIAGNOSTIC SYSTEM"),nl,
```

```
      diagnosed(_),!,nl,clear_facts.
    run:-
      write("\nUnable to determine what"),nl,
      write("your problem is. \n"),clear_facts.
```

2. The following displays all solutions. A test "diagnostic" has been added to show multiple solution capability:

```
/*    AUTOMOTIVE DIAGNOSTIC SYSTEM
          displays all solutions
/*

/* Note: To eliminate a warning on compiling,
     see information in the manual on reference
     objects.  */
database
  xpositive(symbol)
  xnegative(symbol)

predicates
  run
  diagnosed(symbol)
  check(symbol)
  positive(string,symbol)
  negative(string,symbol)
  clear_facts
  remember(symbol,char)
  ask(string,symbol,char)
  go_once(char)

clauses
  run:-
    write("AUTOMOBILE DIAGNOSTIC SYSTEM"),nl,
    go_once(Diagnosed), nl,
    Diagnosed='y',clear_facts.
  run.

  go_once(Diagnosed) :-
    diagnosed(_),Diagnosed='y',fail.

  go_once(_).

  positive(_,Y) if xpositive(Y),!.
  positive(X,Y) if not(xnegative(Y)) and
   ask(X,Y,Reply), Reply='y'.

  negative(_,Y) if xnegative(Y),!.
```

237

```
                    negative(X,Y) if not(xpositive(Y)) and
                     ask(X,Y,Reply), Reply='n'.


                    ask(X,Y,Reply) :-
                      write(X),nl,
                      readchar(Reply),
                      write(Reply),nl,
                      remember(Y,Reply).

                    remember(Y,'y'):-
                      asserta(xpositive(Y)).

                    remember(Y,'n'):-
                      asserta(xnegative(Y)).

                    clear_facts:-
                      retract(xpositive(_)),fail.

                    clear_facts:-
                      retract(xnegative(_)),fail.

                    clear_facts:-
                      nl,nl,write("Please press the space bar to
                       Exit"),nl,
                      readchar(_).

                    diagnosed(starter_motor) :-
                      not(check(engine_turns_over)),
                      check(electrical_power),
                      check(relay),
                      not(check(starter_motor)),
                      write("Replace starter motor."),nl.

                    diagnosed(test) :-
                      not(check(engine_turns_over)),
                      check(relay),
                      not(check(starter_motor)),
                      write("This is a test for multiple
                       solutions."),nl.
                    diagnosed(battery_connections) :-
                      not(check(engine_turns_over)),
                      not(check(electrical_power)),
                      not(check(battery_connections)),
                      write("Tighten battery connections."),nl.

                    diagnosed(battery_water) :-
                      not(check(engine_turns_over)),
```

```
    not(check(electrical_power)),
    check(battery_connections),
    not(check(battery_water)),
    write("Fill battery with water."),nl.

diagnosed(battery_charged) :-
    not(check(engine_turns_over)),
    not(check(electrical_power)),
    check(battery_connections),
    check(battery_water),
    not(check(battery_charged)),
    write("Battery is not charged. Try jumping
      it to start"),nl,
    write("then check for loose or broken fan
      belt or defective"),nl,
    write("regulator."),nl.

diagnosed(relay) :-
    not(check(engine_turns_over)),
    check(electrical_power),
    not(check(relay)),
    write("Check ignition fuse, key switch, and
      starter motor"),nl,
    write("relay."),nl.

diagnosed(spark_delivery_system) :-
    check(engine_turns_over),
    not(check(spark_delivery_system)),
    write("Check distributor, spark plugs, and
      related wiring."),nl.

diagnosed(fuel_system) :-
    check(engine_turns_over),
    check(spark_delivery_system),
    write("Check gas gauge, fuel filter, and
      possibility of"),nl,
    write("flooding."),nl.

check(battery_connections) :-
    positive("Are the battery connections good
      (y/n) ? ",battery_connections).

check(electrical_power) :-
    negative("Are the headlights dim or do they
      fail to light (y/n) ? ",battery_charged).

check(battery_water) :-
    positive("Is the battery water level good
      (y/n) ? ",battery_water).
```

```
check(engine_turns_over) :-
    positive("Does the engine turn over normally
    (y/n) ? ",engine).

check(spark_delivery_system) :-
    positive("Are the spark plug and distributor
    wires good (y/n) ? ",spark).

check(starter_motor) :-
    negative("Does the starter motor fail to
    turn, turn slowly, or grind (y/n) ?
    ",motor).

check(relay) :-
    positive("Can you hear the starter motor
    relay pull in (y/n) ? ",relay).

check(battery_charged) :-
    positive("Is the battery fully charged?
    (y/n) ? ",battery).
```

3. The solution would be the same as example 2 except that a goal section is added as in exercise 1.

4. Not applicable

Chapter 12

1. Not applicable

2. Not applicable

3. There is no clear distinction, but in general an expert system mimics the performance of an expert in a specific domain. A knowledge system uses formal reasoning to solve problems. Both use the same inference engine or control logic—the only difference is the database and the application. A system that analyzes an expense account to determine what can be reimbursed under corporate rules is more like a knowledge system because it doesn't mimic an expert. A medical diagnostic system, in contrast, would be an expert system because it mimics the performance of a doctor in a limited domain.

Chapter 13

1. A flat domain is one in which there is no hierarchy. An address file of a club membership would be flat if no organization roles are included.

2. Not applicable

Chapter 14

1. The *xpositive* and *xnegative* database predicates are the working memory. The *diagnosed* and *check* predicates are the rule base. All other predicates are the inference engine.

2. Advantages: The developer does not need to write much of the inference engine program because it is internal to Prolog. Development time is fast because Prolog is a high-level language. Disadvantages: Prolog is primarily limited to depth-first backward chaining. As a high-level language, it provides less symbolic manipulation capability than a low-level declarative language such as LISP.

Chapter 15

1. Some general methods are:

- Use multichoice questions to prune the search space as quickly as possible.

- Query on symptoms that eliminate approximately half of the unproven goals. For example, in a medical diagnostic system with seven conclusions of which half have a fever symptom, asking if the patient has a fever will give an answer that eliminates half of the conclusions.

- Avoid questions that can lead to blind paths.

2a. Planning systems use forward chaining.

2b. Diagnostic systems use forward chaining, backward chaining, decision trees, or heuristic methods.

2c. Monitoring and control systems use forward chaining.

Chapter 16

1. Define the domain as objectively as possible. Identify the specific conclusions that will be tested in the prototype. Ask the doctor to define the resources you should use to identify the symptoms associated with the specific conclusions.

2. The problem areas include:

- The relationship between symptoms and conclusions is not always certain. Many related symptoms can increase certainty, but a high level of certainty is never assured.

- There may be more than one conclusion, with interrelated symptoms.

- Symptoms can be intermittent and vary with different factors such as stress, nutrition, and physical activity.

- There is no true standard to use for comparison.

- The relationship of some facts may not be known.

3. To reduce the domain and search space:

- Keep the number of supported conclusions as small as possible.
- Try to prune the search space during the consultation as quickly as possible.

4. Symptomatic subgoals could be classed by system: eye, ear, brain and nervous system, teeth and mouth, respiratory system, circulatory system, digestive system, liver and gallbladder, kidneys and urinary system, reproductive system, joints and muscles, and skin. Also, you can subclassify symptoms. For example, if fever is a goal, a high, steady fever would be a subgoal.

Chapter 17

1. Not applicable

2. The number of goal states is defined by the number of things that can go wrong. You can start with a small number of goals (small domain) and gradually expand it. With some systems, even a small number of goals can make an effective system. In other cases, the system is not really productive unless a large number of goals is used. For the computer diagnostic system, the best way to start is to list all the things that could go wrong that a user could fix.

The number of rules is determined by the search space. If a decision tree space is used, with each branch indicating two decisions (a yes or no answer), the number of rules is roughly twice the number of goal states. Good heuristic design can reduce the number of rules used.

3. An example of shallow knowledge is the knowledge of the relationship between the installation of some resident programs and a particular computer fault, such as the inability of the computer to format a disk if certain resident programs are installed. An example of deep knowledge is knowing why the resident programs cause the format program to fail. The deeper knowledge might make it possible to solve the problem more specifically, such as by installing the resident programs in a different order instead of eliminating the programs.

Chapter 18

1. Not applicable

2. Each hypothesis on the original fact list is tested with the facts from the list. If the system is functioning correctly, the matching hypothesis should be reached as a conclusion.

3. Not applicable

Chapter 19

Not applicable

Glossary

ALGORITHM. A procedure that, if followed, guarantees a specified output. With conventional programming, a programmer implements a program that follows a specified algorithm. *See also* HEURISTIC.

ARGUMENT. The parameters of a functor.

ARITY. The number of arguments in a functor.

ARTIFICIAL INTELLIGENCE (AI). "A subfield of computer science concerned with the concepts and methods of symbolic inference by a computer and the symbolic representation of the knowledge used in making inferences. A field aimed at pursuing the possibility that a computer can be made to behave in ways that humans recognize as 'intelligent' behavior in each other" (Feigenbaum and McCorduck).

ATOM. A constant data symbol in standard versions of Prolog. Roughly equivalent to an object of the symbolic data type in Turbo Prolog.

ATTRIBUTES. The properties (qualities) of an object. Attributes have values.

BACKTRACKING. A Prolog process in which the program backs up through a sequence of inferences, usually to try a different path.

BACKWARD CHAINING. A type of reasoning process which begins at a specified goal state and works backward in an attempt to prove the specified goal. *See also* FORWARD CHAINING.

BINDING. The process of assigning a known value to a variable.

BLACKBOARD SYSTEM. An expert system in which several knowledge bases use a common working memory, called a "black-board."

BODY. The antecedent part of a rule. A compound subgoal.

BREADTH-FIRST SEARCHING. A search strategy in which all rules at a particular hierarchy are pursued before moving to the next level. *See also* DEPTH-FIRST SEARCHING.

BREAK. The :- symbol used to designate the IF operation of a rule.

BUILT-IN PREDICATE. *See* STANDARD PREDICATE.

CERTAINTY FACTOR. A numerical value assigned to a relationship that indicates confidence in that relationship. The value can range from 1 to −1. A value of 1 indicates an absolute certainty in the relationship being true and −1 indicates absolute certainty in the relationship being false. Also called confidence factor.

CHUNK. The elementary pattern in perception and thinking. Each rule is a chunk in a rule-based system.

CHUNKING. The organization of related knowledge such that a collection of facts can be treated as a single unit.

CLAUSE. A fact or a rule, followed by a period. A conjunctively related term.

COMPILER. A language tool that parses a source program and stores the data in a more efficient form for later execution.

COMPILED KNOWLEDGE. Knowledge about a domain that is abstracted from an expert and structured into a form that can be used for productive purposes.

Implies chunking, hierarchies, and the defining of relationships between facts.

COMPOUND GOAL. A goal containing at least two subgoals.

COMPOUND STRUCTURE. An object that contains another object in a hierarchical relationship. It is defined by a functor that names the parent object and a list of child objects, separated by commas and enclosed in parentheses.

CONCEPT. A collection of physical or conceptual entities of the same class; the basic unit of knowledge.

CONFIDENCE FACTOR. *See* CERTAINTY FACTOR.

CONFLICT RESOLUTION. In a production system, a way of determining which rule to use when two or more rules unify with the given goal.

CONJUNCTION. The combination of two conditions such that the goal is satisfied only if both of the conditions are satisfied. A conjunction is expressed as an AND operation.

CONSULTATION PARADIGM. A particular user interface in which the user is moved through the problem space to the goal with a series of interactive questions. *See also* PARADIGM.

CUT. A Prolog operator that, when invoked, commits Prolog to use all choices and variable bindings made at that point in the evaluation of the group of clauses (predicates) containing the cut.

DATABASE. A collection of known facts and rules about a domain.

See also Dynamic database, Static database.

Data-driven system. A forward-chaining system.

Decision tree. A network map of the reasoning process of an expert system that shows consultation questions as nodes, and answers as links.

Declarative language. A language in which the knowledge about a domain is expressed in an objective form in a symbolic language. Problems are solved by stating a goal for which the computer must determine an attribute value. Formal algorithms are generally not expressed in the language but heuristics and other knowledge about the procedure may be expressed, from which the computer can determine a path to the specified goal. Example languages include Prolog and LISP.

Deep knowledge. Knowledge of the root causes, theories, and facts about a domain. *See also* Shallow knowledge.

Definitional concept. A concept at any level other than the highest level of a given taxonomy. *See also* Concept, Primitive concept.

Depth-first searching. A search strategy in which all nodes relative to a specific conclusion are pursued as deeply as possible until that conclusion is proven true or false. *See also* Breadth-first searching.

Diagnostic system. A type of expert system used to relate behavioral faults (symptoms) to causes.

Disjunction. The combination of two conditions such that the goal is satisfied if either of the conditions is satisfied. A disjunction is expressed as an OR operation.

Domain. 1. (Turbo Prolog language) The types of values an object may take in a predicate expression. If *day* is typed as an integer, it is of the integer domain. 2. (Representation theory) An objective and definable extent of knowledge about a specified subject matter. Medicine is a broad domain, preventive medicine is a smaller domain, and nutrition is a still smaller domain.

Dynamic database. That part of the database to which facts can be added or removed during program execution. Facts are added using the *asserta* or *assertz* predicate, and removed with the *retract* predicate. *See also* Database, Static database.

Expert system. An intelligent computer program that uses knowledge and inference procedures to solve problems that are difficult enough to require significant human expertise for their solution (Feigenbaum). Also called knowledge system.

Expertise. Skill, knowledge, heuristics, and procedures in a particular domain. This implies not only a knowledge of the domain, but also the ability to organize this knowledge into chunks and networks for practical use.

Explanatory interface module. That part of an expert system that permits the user to query about the reasoning process used in reaching a particular goal state.

FACETS. In a frame-type system, slots that are used to store constraint values for other slots (such as a minimum or maximum value).

FACT. An assertion of truth about an object, or a relationship between objects, such as *is__a(penguin,bird)*. A fact is always terminated by a period. A Prolog program consists of facts and rules.

FIFTH-GENERATION COMPUTERS. Computers that use architecture that is not bound by von Neumann architecture. In general, refers to hardware specifics of expert systems and artificial intelligence, including features such as multiple processors and nonlinear (parallel) processing.

FIRING. The process in a production system inference cycle in which the conclusion is accepted as true (all conditions or subgoals have been proven true), and the conclusion is added to dynamic memory.

FLAT. Any knowledge representation in which there is no hierarchy.

FORMAL REASONING. The process of solving a problem by inference.

FORWARD CHAINING. A type of reasoning process that begins with the known facts and works forward, trying to find a successful goal state. *See also* BACKWARD CHAINING.

FRAME. The basic unit of storage in a frame representation. *See* FRAME REPRESENTATION.

FRAME REPRESENTATION. A type of knowledge representation in which an object is associated with a number of attributes or properties, and the attributes are associated with values. The object is represented by a frame, the attributes by slots in the frame, and the values are stored in the slots.

FUNCTOR. The relationship part of a predicate or the parent object of a compound structure.

GOAL. One or more relations, each involving objects or variables, that a Prolog program must attempt to solve.

GOAL-DIRECTED SYSTEM. A backward-chaining system.

GOAL STATE. A specified attribute and value (or object, attribute, and value) that can be satisfied with the given facts and rules.

HEAD. 1. The conclusion part of a rule. 2. The first item of a list.

HEURISTIC. A rule of thumb or other device that reduces the problem space for a specific problem solution. Heuristics do not guarantee a solution, nor (if a solution exists) do they guarantee the most efficient path to a solution. *See also* ALGORITHM.

HIERARCHY. An ordered network in which some objects are subordinate to others. Hierarchies imply inheritance. Objects at the higher level are the parent, and objects immediately subordinate are the children.

HIGH-LEVEL LANGUAGE. A computer language in which a single instruction represents many instructions in computer code. FORTRAN, BASIC, and

COBOL are all high-level languages.

INFERENCE. A process in which new facts are derived from known facts using rules and modens ponens.

INFERENCE ENGINE. That part of an expert system that infers new facts from existing facts using rules in the database, and also controls the flow and order of the inference.

INFIX NOTATION. Expressions in which the operator is between the operands or values on which it operates. *See also* PREFIX NOTATION.

INHERITANCE. A process in which attribute values of one object are assumed as attribute values of another. If we assume a bird has wings and a sparrow is a bird, we can assume a sparrow has wings. The object *sparrow* inherits the *has wings* property of *bird*.

INSTANTIATE. To bind a variable. To assign a value to a variable.

INTERPRETER. A language tool in which the source code is parsed, converted to an executable form, and then executed immediately. *See also* COMPILER.

KNOWLEDGE. Facts and relationships about a particular domain that can be used to solve problems in that domain.

KNOWLEDGE ACQUISITION MODULE. That part of an expert system that permits new rules and facts to be added to the static database (or rule base).

KNOWLEDGE BASE. The rules and facts that a Prolog program uses to solve a particular problem. It

consists of the rule base and working memory. The rule base corresponds to the Prolog static database, and working memory corresponds to the dynamic database. *See also* RULE BASE, WORKING MEMORY, DYNAMIC MEMORY, STATIC MEMORY.

KNOWLEDGE ENGINEER. An individual who specializes in accessing problems that normally require the skill of an expert, acquiring knowledge, and then developing representational systems. One who builds expert systems.

KNOWLEDGE SYSTEM. *See* Expert system.

LISP. One of the leading languages for knowledge engineers and AI researchers. For AI programming, LISP is normally considered a low-level language. It is more difficult to use, and a program in LISP requires more instructions than a similar program in a higher-level language (such as Prolog or one using expert system shells). At the same time, however, it provides more power for the user in terms of inference control and knowledge representation.

LIST. An object that consists of an ordered set of elements.

MATCH. The process of comparing functors, arities, and arguments of a goal with a fact or the head of a rule. Unification involves both matching and binding. *See* UNIFICATION.

METARULE. A rule about other rules.

MODENS PONENS. A rule of logic that asserts that if *A* implies *B* and *A* is true, *B* is true.

MONOTONIC REASONING. A reasoning system in which a fact or conclusion, after it is added to the dynamic database (working memory), cannot be removed during the course of a particular consultation.

MYCIN. An expert system, developed at Stanford during the mid-seventies, that was designed to aid physicians in the diagnosis and treatment of meningitis and bacteremia infections. MYCIN is often referred to as the first of the productive and useful expert systems.

NATURAL LANGUAGE. A branch of AI that studies techniques that allow computers to accept input and produce output in conventional languages such as English.

NONMONOTONIC REASONING. A reasoning system in which facts and conclusions can be added or removed from working memory (dynamic database) during a consultation.

OBJECT. 1. (Turbo Prolog object) Any element of a predicate. 2. (Representational theory) Any physical or conceptual entity that can have one or more attributes.

OBJECT-ATTRIBUTE-VALUE (O-A-V) TRIPLET. A type of tabular knowledge representation in which knowledge is represented by objects. Each object has one or more attributes, and the attributes have values. In simpler systems, attribute-value (A-V) pairs may be used.

OBJECT LANGUAGE. A declarative language in which the knowledge in the domain is expressed as knowledge about objects. The objects have attributes, and the attributes have values.

PARADIGM. Problem-solving scenario that is specific for a general base of applications. A diagnostic/prescriptive consultation paradigm is one of the most common paradigms.

PARSING. The process of breaking down an expression into its component symbols and determining the syntax. *See* SYNTAX.

PREDICATE. A function that has a value of true or false and expresses a property or relationship.

PREDICTION SYSTEM. A type of knowledge system that predicts a future goal state from a given state.

PREFIX NOTATION. Expressions in which the operator precedes the operands or values on which it operates. *See also* INFIX NOTATION.

PRIMITIVE CONCEPT. A concept at the highest level of a given taxonomy. It has no parent, and cannot be defined in absolute terms. *See also* CONCEPT, DEFINITIONAL CONCEPT.

PROBLEM SPACE. A network consisting of the nodes and links for the solution of problems in a specified domain. The nodes represent goals and subgoals that are a part of the solution process. The links represent operations, or pathways between the goals and subgoals. Also called search space.

PROCEDURAL LANGUAGE. A language in which an algorithm for solving a problem is expressed in an objective form and can be used repeatedly to solve a variety of problems that can be addressed by the same algorithm. Example languages include Pascal, C, BASIC, and COBOL.

PRODUCTION. A rule; the basic unit of storage in a rule-based system.

PRODUCTION SYSTEM. *See* RULE-BASED SYSTEM.

PROLOG. A very popular expert system language that is primarily oriented to depth-first, backward-chaining reasoning.

PROPERTY. A specific quality or attribute of an object. Properties have values.

PROPERTY LIST. A database structure in which properties are associated with objects. Property lists are used to create frame representations.

PROPOSITION. An expression that affirms or denies something about an object.

PROTOTYPE. A preliminary version of an expert system, usually representing a much smaller domain than the final system.

PRUNING. The process of reducing the search space by removing one or more branches of the decision tree.

REASONING. The process of using rules to infer new facts from existing facts.

RECURSION. A technique in which an entity is defined in terms of itself. In Prolog, a recursive clause is a clause defined in terms of itself.

RELATION. A name describing the way in which a collection of objects (or objects and variables)

belong together. The functor part of a predicate.

ROLE. Components of an object or concept. Objects have properties and roles. Roles, like properties, can have values (for example, car → wheels → 4).

RULE. A clause that expresses a relationship between facts. A rule is a conditional statement of two parts. The first part is called the head, hypothesis, conclusion, or proposition. The second part is called the body, premise, or antecedent. The two parts are connected by an IF operator. Each condition of the antecedent and the conclusion are usually expressed as a form of object attribute-value triplets or attribute-value pairs.

RULE BASE. That part of an expert system that is used to store static information about a domain (knowledge that does not change during a particular consultation). The rule base corresponds to the Prolog static database. *See* STATIC DATABASE.

RULE-BASED SYSTEM. A type of knowledge representation in which knowledge about a domain is expressed in rules that describe relationships between facts.

RUNTIME SYSTEM. An expert system that can run independent of the development language. If the development language is a compiler, the source code can easily be compiled to a runtime system that no longer needs the development language and in which the source code is protected (not available to the user). If the development language is an interpreter or shell, the user may need a support module to run the expert system and will need to pay the associated cost of the module. If you are developing an expert system for retail sale, you will need to investigate the cost of any runtime support the user will need. With Turbo Prolog, you can compile to a runtime system that requires no additional software on the part of the user.

SCRIPT. A frame-type knowledge structure that is used to represent a sequence of events. The slots contain event related data, and are linked in a chain.

SEARCH SPACE. *See* PROBLEM SPACE.

SEMANTICS. The interpretation or meaning of an expression. *See also* SYNTAX.

SEMANTIC NETWORK. A network type of knowledge representation in which objects and values are represented as nodes, and relations are represented as links.

SHALLOW KNOWLEDGE. Knowledge about a domain that permits inferences to be made when the deeper causes and theories are not known. The human brain does not distinguish between shallow and deep knowledge, but utilizes all knowledge available, as appropriate, to make decisions. Also called surface knowledge. *See also* DEEP KNOWLEDGE.

SHELL. A very high-level expert system language that permits the construction of very powerful systems with a minimum of programming. The knowledge engineer can concentrate on the knowledge and knowledge rela-

tionships without having to be concerned with inference control and other programming aspects. At the same time, however, the user is limited to whatever features and inferences control the shell supports.

SLOT. Object storage unit in a frame-type system. Slots can contain the object's name, properties (attributes), values, default values, limits for other values, procedures to determine values, rules to determine values, pointers to other frames, or any other object related knowledge.

STANDARD PREDICATE. A predicate that is integral to a specific Prolog implementation.

STATE. A node in a problem space.

STATIC DATABASE. That part of the database that remains constant during program execution. *See also* DATABASE, DYNAMIC DATABASE.

STATIC FRAME. A frame in which the attribute values do not change during the course of a consultation.

SUBGOAL. A goal that is part of another goal.

SURFACE KNOWLEDGE. *See* SHALLOW KNOWLEDGE.

SYMBOL. A sign used to represent objects, concepts, operations, relationships, or object properties (attributes). Any component of a knowledge structure.

SYNTAX. Defines the order of the symbols in an expression. Computers are good at resolving syntax, but do poorly in interpreting semantics. *See* SEMANTICS.

TAIL. The part of the list that remains if the head is taken away. The tail of a list with a single item is an empty list ([]).

TAXONOMY. A system of arranging objects into natural, related groups based on some factor common to each. Normally implies a hierarchical class relationship and inheritance.

TERM. A Turbo Prolog object, list, or compound structure.

TRIGGERING. The process in a production system in which a rule is selected for processing. The unification with the head has been accomplished and the inference engine is processing each condition of the antecedent.

UNIFICATION. A process in which Prolog tries to match a subgoal against facts and heads of other rules to prove the subgoal.

VALUE. The quantity or quality of an attribute. Objects have attributes, and attributes have values.

VARIABLE. A name used to represent a value. A variable always begin with an uppercase letter.

VON NEUMANN ARCHITECTURE. A type of computer design in which a single block of memory is used for both program and data. Programs execute linearly using instructions stored in sequential memory locations.

WINDOWING. The sectioning of the display screen into one or more viewing areas to permit you to view simultaneously different types of data. Turbo Prolog permits the construction of windows.

WORKING MEMORY. That part of the expert system that is used to store facts and conclusions relating to a specific consultation. Working memory corresponds to the Prolog dynamic database. *See* DYNAMIC DATABASE.

Bibliography

Clocksin, W.F., and C.S. Mellish. *Programming in Prolog*. Berlin: Springer-Verlag, 1984.
   This is the classic text on Prolog, and defines the language. Turbo Prolog differs somewhat from this C&M version, but this book is still an important reference for Prolog work.

Covington, Michael. "Programming in Logic." *PC Technical Journal* 3 (December 1985).
   This article, the first of a two-part article on Prolog, is a tutorial. The second article, which reviews available versions of Prolog on personal computers, is in the next month's issue.

Cuadrado, Clara Y., and John Cuadrado, "Prolog Goes to Work." *BYTE* 10 (August 1985): 151-158.
   Description of using Prolog to implement an adventure-type game, with a good overview of Prolog research.

Forsyth, Richard. *Expert Systems: Principles and Case Studies*. London: Chapman and Hall, 1984.
   Overview of expert systems, with particular emphasis on rule-based systems and methods for dealing with uncertainty. Not language specific.

Godenberg, Janet. "Experts on Call." *PC WORLD* 3 (September 1985): 192-199.
   Overview of expert system shells available for the PC.

Harmon, Paul, and David King. *Expert Systems: Artificial Intelligence in Business*. New York: John Wiley & Sons, 1985.
   Practical overview of expert systems including extensive review of current systems and tools. Not language specific.

Hayes-Roth et al. *Building Expert Systems*. Reading, MA: Addison Wesley, 1983.
   This remains a classic text for expert system development. Somewhat LISP oriented.

Townsend, Carl, and Dennis Feucht. *Personal Expert Systems: Designing and Programming.* Blue Ridge Summit, PA: Tab, 1985.

This is a tutorial on personal computer expert systems and contains the source code for a FORTH inference engine for expert system experimenting.

Winston, Patrick Henry. *Artificial Intelligence.* 2ed. Reading: Addison-Wesley, 1984.

This is a classic text on artificial intelligence, with emphasis on the LISP language. Some material on production systems.

General

AI Expert. PO Box 10952, Palo Alto, CA, 94303-9908.

This is a new magazine directed to the more practical aspects of expert system development. Premier issue has a good review of Turbo Prolog.

Computer Language. 2443 Fillmore Street, Suite #346, San Francisco, CA, 94115.

This excellent magazine is for programmers, and covers many languages. Watch for issues on AI and articles on Prolog and LISP.

The AI Magazine and AAAI Conference Proceedings. The AAAI, 445 Burgess Drive, Menlo Park, CA, 94025-3496.

Technical publications for programmers and knowledge engineers.

Association for Computing Machinery, 11 West 42nd Street, New York, NY, 10036.

Technical publication for programmers and knowledge engineers.

Byte 10 (April 1985).

This entire issue is on artificial intelligence. Although the emphasis is primarily on LISP, there are several good articles, including John Steven's "Reverse Engineering the Brain" and two articles on expert systems.

PC 4 (August 1985).

This entire issue is on expert system shells. Although you will not find anything on Prolog, you will find extensive reviews of several expert system shells for the personal computer.

A public domain Prolog interpreter is available through many user groups. You can order it as disk #417 for $6.00, plus $4.00 shipping, from PC-SIG, 1030 E. Duane, Suite J, Sunnyvale, CA, 94086. The disk also contains many excellent Prolog examples.

A Prolog tutorial is available for $49.95 USA funds from Logicware, 5915 Airport Rd, Mississauga, Ontario, Canada, L4V 1T1 or by calling 416-672-0300. This is an excellent self-teaching program with over 400 pages of tutorial material and two computer-aided tutorial program disks that run on an IBM PC. The tutorial illustrates basic Prolog principles, particularly backtracking and the cut. You can step through the sample program executions. You do not need Prolog to use the tutorial, because a limited version of Prolog is integrated into the system. Although the tutorial is oriented toward the MPROLOG version (which the company sells), it has material that applies to Turbo Prolog as well.

Index